A Memoir

WHAT
ARE
YOU?

The Unfolding Story
of a 1943 Bi-ethnic Adoption

Dr. June P. Murray

Published by
123 Mango Tree LLC
PO Box 376
Ladson, SC 29456-0376
www.123MangoTree.com

Summary: This riveting memoir is about a bi-ethnic woman whose Irish/Catholic birthmother made arrangements for her to be privately adopted by a bi-ethnic married couple in 1943. The memoir details the author's experiences as an adopted child including her extraordinary encounters with racism.

ISBN 9781087938592 (hardback)
Library of Congress Control Number: 2021934443

[1. Memoir—Nonfiction. 2. Adoption—Nonfiction 3. Bi-ethnic adoption—Nonfiction.]

10 9 8 7 6 5 4 3 2 1

Printed in the United States of America

DEDICATION

The very existence of my life happened because of my birthmother Shirley O'Mara Cushen, and a missing link—my birthfather, who may have never known about his role. To these individuals, I truly owe my life. I thank Shirley, to whom I owe the utmost gratitude for bringing me into this world, and for knowing and understanding who best should nurture my life. She not only knew these things, but she made them happen by working very closely with Agnes and Andrew Murray. To those extraordinary two people I owe my *everything*—all that makes me moral, all that makes me confident, all that makes me happy, all that I have learned about the need for harmony in life and the truly important lessons of living a good life. So thank you Mommy and Daddy. I am and always will be completely indebted to you. Therefore, this book, the true and most remarkable story of your decision to adopt me and all that decision entailed, is dedicated to you.

INTRODUCTION

In 1943, the State of Connecticut officially allowed private adoptions to take place between birthmothers and married couples. The signature of the husband of the birthmother is how the father of the child was determined, or it could be the man the birthmother designated as the father. This process existed many years before DNA testing.

This memoir is about a multicultural, multiethnic, and multi-religious adoption during World War II. The adoption was between the birthmother, her legal husband (who was not the biological father of the child), and a married couple. It was the last private adoption permitted in Connecticut for another 35 years.

The book details the extensive plans to maintain the privacy of everyone involved and the near failure of the adoption process. This story includes how the adoption occurred and details the lives of the key people involved. It captures how the child learned she was adopted, and how she dealt with her many cultures and ethnicities. The story also explores a mystery that occurred when the child was almost five years of age.

The book may serve as a guide for those thinking about adopting. It may also stimulate memories or questions for those who have been adopted.

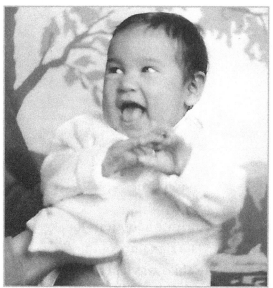

June at 3 months old

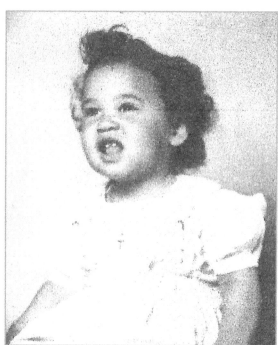

June at 1 year

June at 1 year with mother Agnes

June at age 7 with sister, Cathy, age 2

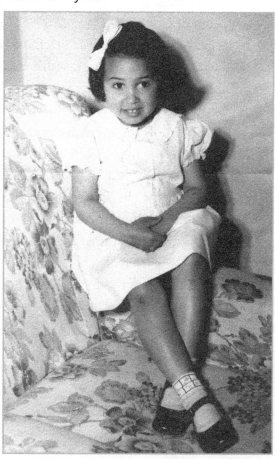

June at age 4

CHAPTER ONE
Looking back on understanding
I was adopted: Phase One

My parents sought the help of a child psychologist to help me understand that I was adopted. I met with him for six months. I was nine years old on the day of my last session. I heard him tell my mother I "knew that I was adopted" but "not to press me or try to discuss the matter with me" because I wasn't emotionally ready to accept that I was adopted.

My mother just couldn't follow his instructions. As soon as we were in the car, she began urging me to discuss my adoption. "So you know that you were adopted, right?" she asked.

This made me angry and frightened. I refused to answer and turned my face to the car window for the rest of the way home. The scenery along the Boston Post Road between New Haven and Milford was a blur. I was afraid she would begin the dreaded conversation once we arrived home, so I stayed outside—alone—waiting for my father to come home from work.

Finally, I heard the tires of my father's car crunching the pebble driveway along the side of our home. He smiled and waved at me as usual, but the smile on his face turned to an expression of puzzled concern. I guessed it was because normally, I would've bounced over to the edge of the lawn as he drove into the backyard waving and calling, "Hi, Daddy!" Then I would've begun chattering away about items of interest to me, which I felt would also interest him. But on this day, I stood in the middle of the yard next to his favorite lawn chair quietly waiting for him to come out of the detached garage. The car door slammed and I watched him swing the garage doors shut. He walked over to me and looked down at my face with concern. I didn't need him to ask me what was wrong because his expression of interest and closeness was all I needed.

I launched right in and said, "Daddy! Dr. Kleeman said I was adopted! Mommy said so too. I wasn't adopted, was I Daddy? That's not true, is it?" I pleaded and demanded at the same time.

My father gazed at me in a steady, expressionless manner for what seemed like an eternity. He broke his silence by smiling the devilish grin he was famous for. He placed his arm around my shoulders and turned me around to face our back door. "No, of course not!" he said. "Now come on, let's go inside and see if dinner is ready."

I immediately felt a sense of relief from the gripping fear brought on by the knowledge that I was adopted. Some of my fear stemmed from feeling there was a reason my parents kept my adoption a secret for so long. I remember feeling like my life was threatened from existence—that Mommy and Daddy weren't my Mommy and Daddy and if that was so then who was I? I was scared that I would be alone because learning I was adopted followed the trauma of previously being sent away from my original home.

Later, I learned my mother called my father as soon as we arrived home. She told him what the psychologist's recommendations were and how I reacted when she tried to discuss my adoption with me. So my wise, gentle, and caring father gave me a reprieve. He knew that even though I understood I was adopted, I wasn't emotionally ready to accept that reality.

As a result, a large pink elephant sat between my mother, father, and me for the next four years—the period of time I needed to come to grips with the truth that I was an adopted child.

TRYING TO ACCEPT THE TRUTH: PHASE TWO

After I learned about my adoption from the psychologist, I tried to accept it during the following four years. I would play mind games with myself. Some days I would say to myself, *you're adopted you know*. Then I would respond to myself, *ohhh no…I'm not!*

If my younger sister, Cathy, did something I found particularly annoying, I would say to myself *who cares*. There's no blood relation between us! If my parents and I locked horns on some issue, I would sulk in my room and think,

I hope it is true that I am adopted! And when the reality of my adoption occurred to me every now and then, I thought well believe it because it's true!

Between the ages of nine and thirteen, my parents indirectly tried to help me accept my adoption. Their circle of friends included a couple that had an adopted daughter exactly my age. Her name was Barbara and we became very good friends.

My parents would make comments like, "you know, Barbara was adopted and her parents love her so much. They treat her just like they treat Wesley (her brother). No one would know that Barbara was adopted!"

I eventually learned that Barbara's parents were using the same strategy to help her accept being adopted as well. One day when we were twelve, Barbara and I were complaining about how awful our parents were—probably because of the normal restrictions they placed on us or the chores they required us to do. I got up enough nerve to say something to her that I had been thinking a lot about for a long time. I said, "Well, I know something about you and your parents."

Without batting an eye, she responded, "Yeah! Well, I know something about you too!" She went on to say, "Maybe you heard that I was adopted! Well, I know that you were adopted too!"

I was shocked. There it was! Out! The mind games would become far more difficult to play now. The truth laid bare before me and God and the world. Still, I wasn't prepared to discuss my adoption with my parents or to hear about how it developed. The reasons why any child would be adopted and why they were given away by their birthparents were still threatening to me. The unknown was frightening. I feared that my biological parents didn't want me. I feared learning the answers to the questions that came to mind such as, *what was so wrong with me that made my real parents not want me* and *who am I really*.

About another year passed by after this conversation with Barbara. Then one night my parents attended the wake of one of my father's oldest friends. He was a very close member of our family village who had died suddenly. I was left at home to babysit Cathy who was eight years old at the time. I was engaged in one of my self-pampering routines—taking a bubble bath and luxuriating in scented suds—when my sister burst into the bathroom with a tiny newspaper clipping in her hand.

"Look!" she exclaimed, "Your name was in the newspaper only they have the last name for you wrong. But Mom and Dad's name is correct!"

She handed me the newspaper clipping and I read it. This was the first time I had seen anything related to my adoption in writing. The clipping was the June 1943 newspaper article that was the official notice of my pending adoption. My sister had found it tucked away in a book on a shelf in our living room. The article listed my biological mother's married name as my last name, which was my legal name until my adoption was final. This clipping was the truth written in black and white. The mind games I played were no longer possible. The evidence of the truth was in my hand, which meant it was time for my parents and me to have that dreaded conversation.

I knew that my sister didn't understand the significance of the clipping, so I wasn't angry with her for finding it. I was annoyed that in addition to confronting the evidence of my adoption, I had to pick up the books she had littered over the living room floor and place them back on the shelf. And because of my mother's obsessive manner and demand for cleanliness, I had to place them in a particular order.

As the night went on, I remember feeling emotionally stressed and angry. I don't know whether that anger was about being adopted; seeing the fact in print and no longer being able to deny it; or if it was an expression of my adolescent rebellion. All I know is that I chose to defy my parents by not doing some chore they had left for me to do. Then, as my Dad would put it, "gave some lip" about not doing it after they came back home that evening.

I stomped up the stairs after an angry exchange with my mother. My father followed me and told me to go downstairs and apologize for speaking disrespectfully to her. Now, you have to understand, I never sassed my father. We rarely had conflicts and when on the rare occasions he had to chastise me, he did it with humor and made the situation less tense. But this time, I wheeled around and screamed at him, "Don't you tell me what to do! You aren't even my father and I know it now!"

I can't bear to describe what my father's face looked like as he heard me scream those words at him. I knew I had hurt him tremendously. I saw it all over his face as his body slumped. If ever in my lifetime there were words that I wish I could take back and had never even uttered, those very words stand out in my mind as if they were written on a red neon sign in a dark night's starless sky.

My father went back to the kitchen to tell my mother what I had said. I sat down on the stairs and burst into tears because on the other side of my anger was pain. My mother rushed to my side and hugged me. We sat there and cried together for a long time.

My father called us into the kitchen where he had made each of us a cup of tea. Gradually and gently, my parents told me the story of my adoption. During the next forty years as my story unfolded, I learned they only told me a very tiny part that night. What is significant about this unfolding process is that for almost eighteen of those years, the voice sharing my adoption story with me belonged to my birthmother, Shirley O'Mara Cushen.

But I am getting ahead of myself. I think it would be helpful to share pertinent background details about my parents—how they met, married, decided to adopt a child, and were further blessed with a biological child.

I also think it's important to clarify that whenever I tell the story of my adoption, I always refer to Agnes and Andrew Murray, the two wonderful people who adopted me, as my mother and father for that is exactly who they were. When I refer to the strong and courageous woman who gave birth to me and had the love, concern, and emotional capability necessary for arranging my adoption, I refer to her as my birthmother or by her name, Shirley.

June's father, Andrew, in his favorite yard chair

Catherine Douglass, June's paternal grandmother's engagement photo, 1896

George Thompson Murray, June's paternal grandfather's engagement photo, 1896

Catherine Douglass on the wedding day, with her sister Lucy and cousin Jane as attendants. The lace on their gowns was made by Catherine.

Chapter Two
My Father's Story

WHO WAS ANDREW MURRAY?

My father, Andrew Douglass Murray, was born in New Haven, Connecticut on March 1, 1903. He was the younger of two surviving children born to Catherine Douglass and George Thompson Murray.

There is a long history between the Murray and Douglass families. In the 1800s, my father's great-grand parents on the Murray and Douglass sides were children during slavery. There were two Scot-Irish sisters who married two Scot-Irish men. One married a Mr. Murray and the other married a Mr. Douglas. These two men owned neighboring plantations in the Salisbury area of North Carolina—not far from Greensboro. The people held in bondage on these two plantations were given the name of the plantation owners. The enslaved families worked for each plantation owner from time to time. Thereby, they came to know everyone who lived on each plantation.

Despite the common rules of the day, the Murray and Douglas plantation owners allowed marriages among those whom they held in bondage. Several of the Murray and Douglass couples married and bore children. Many members of both families worked with the plantation owners as valets, housekeepers, and seamstresses. This allowed them to learn about the fine household furnishings around them like the china, linen, silver, and artwork.

The plantation owners also allowed the men in these two families to work off the plantations and keep a portion of their earnings. Many of the men became members of the clergy, merchants, and carpenters while the women worked as seamstresses and midwives.

In 1840, the senior males in the two families had earned enough to purchase their freedom and that of several adults and children in their family. A large group of Murrays and Douglasses left Salisbury and headed northeast. They traveled to Norfolk, Virginia and settled there. However, the Commonwealth of Virginia passed a law stating that free Blacks had to leave or they would be returned into bondage. The situation was dangerous because bounty hunters would steal any Black person who seemed to be "free" and sell them into slavery. So the Murrays and the Douglasses pulled up stakes once again and continued north.

They made their way towards New England where they could live as free people. Two single Murray men remained in the Baltimore, Maryland area, and two single Douglass men stayed behind in New Jersey. The rest of the group settled between New Haven, Connecticut and New Bedford, Massachusetts. They traveled back and forth between these two states, keeping in touch with one another over the next seventy-five years.

My father's parents, Catherine Douglas and George Murray, were born in Connecticut. They were a middle-class family who were very dedicated to their faith. Their parents helped found and built St. Luke's Church, which was the first African American Episcopal Church built in the State of Connecticut. My grandfather George and his brother, Charlie, built and hand-carved religious symbols into the wooden pews and church altar. The stained-glass windows at the front of the church are in tribute to my father's maternal grandparents, Abbie Douglass and Samuel Thompson Murray, Sr. Over time, my father's parents and their siblings were baptized in St. Luke's, and in 1896 George and Catherine were married there.

Two years after Catherine and George were married, Catherine had a miscarriage then she gave birth to my uncle, Douglass Thompson, on July 2, 1900. She had a daughter, Lucy, one year after Douglass, but little Lucy died at three months old. My father, Andrew, was born two years later. Sadly, Catherine died in June of 1903 when my father was only three months old. Many family members stated that childbirth caused her death, however, she died from tuberculosis. It's worth mentioning that many years later, my father had two daughters who were born in June. It seems to me as if his mother sent us to him.

My father and his brother experienced an extreme sense of loss from which they never fully recovered. His mother was beautiful and the belle of the family. Everyone loved and cherished everything about her. She sang well, played the piano beautifully, and was well read. She was dedicated to the church and was the epitome of grace and loveliness. It was a terrible loss to the Douglass and Murray families.

As a result of his mother's death, Andrew's childhood was marked with emotional suffering. Catherine's husband, my grandfather, never recovered from his loss and was emotionally unavailable to his motherless sons. He relied on his sisters and parents, and his deceased wife's parents to take care of them. They raised the two little boys with the Victorian Era traditions in the High Order of the Episcopalian Church of St. Luke's. They followed strict rules of decorum, learned to be gentlemen, and adhered to the rules of etiquette. They regularly attended church and Sunday school and were taught to have extreme devotion to their church. Still there was little nurturance or affection expressed towards them, especially my father whom they blamed for his mother's death.

Andrew and his brother, Douglas, attended the public elementary school in New Haven. They were sent to boarding school for their middle and high school education. When my father returned to New Haven, he enrolled in a trade school and learned to be a printer. Uncle Doug enlisted in the Navy during World War I. He later attended Tufts University for undergraduate school then Tufts Dental School.

Even though Uncle Doug was a medical professional, he had limited earning potential due to racism. He worked for many years in the school system of Bluefield, Kentucky, practicing dentistry from a mobile unit. Meanwhile, as a blue-collar worker, my father opened his own printing business and earned enough to enable him to live comfortably.

My father also inherited his family's real estate business, and managed the rental of several houses around New Haven. Uncle Doug thought such work was beneath him and was never interested in it. Unfortunately, they let go of the one house I would've been interested in owning. It was a beautiful Victorian house on Martha's Vineyard that the Murrays and Douglasses bought together in the late 1800's for summer retreats. After a while, the elders tired of its upkeep and their children weren't interested in maintaining it. So they stopped paying the taxes on the property. In 1969, I went to the Office of Deeds in Oaks Bluff to look up the house after I heard my father talking about it. I saw a photo of the house taken in 1898 as well as the names on the Deed and saw that it did belong to our family. The house was destroyed to make room to enlarge the current pier for the ferry from Woods Hole to Oak Bluffs. This was not an example of Black people losing property due to eminent domain, but just losing interest and letting it go. What a loss.

The Murray and Douglass families had a long-standing tradition of entrepreneurship. My father's interest in owning a business was inspired by his father and his father's brother, Charles. They opened the first African American owned general store in the state of Connecticut when they were young men. The family owned other businesses such as real estate and was known for being excellent carpenters and members of the clergy.

My father ended up owning three houses besides the one he lived in. He was a much sought after bachelor, but he refrained from becoming seriously involved with the belles of New Haven. He felt that they were more interested in his name and income then in him until he met my mother, Agnes.

C. A. MURRAY & COMPANY,
103 DIXWELL AVENUE,
Cor. Eaton Street,
DEALERS IN
Fine Quality of Meats,
Groceries,   Best Teas and Coffees,
Fine Creamery Butter,
Delicatessen,
FRUITS AND VEGETABLES.
SOUTHERN PRODUCTS.

Telephone.   Delivery.

Advertisement in a recital program for June's paternal Great Uncle Charlie's and his brother (her Paternal Grandfather) George's store.

St. Luke's Episcopal Church, founded in 1845, the first African American Episcopal Church in Connecticut

Stain glass windows in St. Luke's in tribute to Andrew's grandparents

June's paternal uncle Douglass Thompson Murray at age 15 in his WWI U.S. Navy uniform, 1915

Andrew Douglass Murray's high school graduation photo, New Haven, CT, 1921

Andrew and his group of friends, 1935

Andrew with family pet cat "Skeeter," 1938

Andrew with his car that he loaned out to friends, 1938

James Briaca – June's maternal grandfather, Springfield, MA

Theresa Briaca – June's maternal grandmother, Springfield, MA

Agnes, New Haven, CT, 1938

Agnes during her first year of marriage, New Haven, CT, 1939

CHAPTER THREE
My Mother's Story

WHO WAS AGNES BRIACA MURRAY?

My mother's family was very poor. She was the second child and second daughter of five children. She was born in 1917 to Italian, Catholic immigrants, James and Theresa Briaca. They lived in a working-class neighborhood of Springfield, Massachusetts.

Agnes' father, James Briaca, Sr., was a hard drinker and physically and emotionally abusive. He was usually unemployed, which forced his wife, Theresa, to work as a domestic to support the family. James refused to allow Theresa and their children to speak Italian, wanting them to assimilate into the American culture. However, Theresa never mastered the English language and would speak to my mother in Italian whenever James was not at home. My mother became bilingual and was very interested in her mother's Calabrian heritage as well as her own Italian-American heritage.

I learned from my mother and her godmother that Theresa had migrated alone from Calabria during very hard economic times in Italy. The year is uncertain, but my mother thought it might have been 1914 when Theresa was 29 years old. She shared with my mother how hard life was and that her decision to leave Italy was difficult, but it was easier than trying to survive in Calabria. After leaving Italy, Theresa never saw any members of her immediate family again. Her childhood friend, Agatha, also found her way to America and settled in Springfield. Agatha became my mother's godmother and from whom my mother got her first name.

Theresa was a very talented seamstress. I always found this interesting because my father's great grandmother and some of his great aunts were also seamstresses, using their skills to help purchase their freedom. Their family praised them for their talents as opposed to the disdain Theresa sustained from her husband. I never saw any of the outfits my grandmother made for her five children, but one can see the beautiful lace work in my paternal grandmother's wedding dress, as well as the dresses her two bridal attendants wore on that day. I was pleased to inherit my Grandmother Theresa's Singer sewing machine, which I used to make my maternity clothes and most of the clothes my children wore when they were toddlers.

My mother's father, James, migrated to America in 1910 with two of his brothers. Their family owned a farm on the outskirts of Florence, Italy, but it didn't generate enough income to provide for their expanding family. When the opportunity came for them to board a ship and head towards America, they eagerly accepted it. They didn't experience the hardships Theresa faced because it was easier for males to immigrate and travel in the bowels of a large ship.

James and Theresa met through the church in their Springfield neighborhood. They married because they wanted to have a family and begin the process of American citizenship.

James never let Theresa forget her meager beginnings in Calabria, or that she was the only one of her family to migrate to America. Yet he rarely held employment or rose to the financial level his family of origin had in Florence, Italy. He also never became as successful as his two brothers who built a farm in the outskirts of Springfield and did quite well selling produce to the local markets from 1913 through the 1950s.

My mother's father had a haughty attitude and a condescending demeanor. James believed his wife was a peasant so he felt justified in treating her badly. My mother described her father as someone who thought he was too good to work on a farm but not too good to depend on his wife's earnings from domestic work.

He was also racist. He demeaned Theresa because she was doing the same hard work for wealthy Irish families that their African American neighbors were doing. He would criticize his wife then add, "she wasn't better than the neighbors," whom he referred to in a most disrespectful manner. Agnes' father never seemed to realize that her best friend was an African American girl named Deborah. She lived across the street and went to school with Agnes from first grade through high school. Agnes learned how deep racism ran in her community one Saturday when she and Deborah planned to go to the movies. Agnes' mother reminded her that she had to go to their church for confession. So Agnes told Deborah they had to make that quick stop on their way to the movie. They sat in a pew and waited for Agnes' turn with the Priest. An associate Priest entered the Sanctuary and rushed over to Deborah, calling her a derogatory name. He told her she had to leave the church immediately and that "you people aren't welcome here."

Agnes' response was to tell the Priest that Deborah was with her. Being only 13, she thought that would make a difference. Soon she realized it didn't matter why Deborah was in the church or with whom. Under no circumstances would she nor anyone else of her ethnicity be welcome in that church.

My mother told me that story many times as she sought to prepare me for the racism she knew I would experience. She also shared that from that day on, she refused to participate in her mother and father's church or religion. She also admitted that being an Episcopalian wasn't that different from being Catholic because she experienced racism in my father's church as well. How ironic.

James' negative attitude and violent, abusive behavior taught my mother to be open to diversity. She learned to not judge others based on their ethnicity, language skills, nation of origin, or religion. She strived to learn as much as she could about others from different backgrounds.

During the 1920's when my mother was a young child, Springfield, Massachusetts was ethnically and culturally diverse. Her friends were White (Irish and Italian), Black, and Jewish. When I reflect upon my mother's formative years, I realize she was always open to interacting with people who were different from her. She was eager to learn, travel, explore, and expand her mind. I am certain that I inherited these traits from her.

These early traits that my mother developed occurred in contrast to her father's culturally biased orientation. He adhered to an old-fashioned cultural norm in which Italians primarily clustered with other Italians who came from the same part of Italy. My grandfather berated his wife because she was from Calabria, and my mother often shared that he referred to her as a "peasant."

I also find it interesting that as much as my grandfather was upset about my mother marrying an African American, none of my mother's siblings married an Italian. Her oldest sister married a man of Welsh heritage, the next sister married a Scot, her youngest sister married an Irish man, and her only brother married a woman of Polish heritage. My grandfather wanted his children to only speak English so that they could be "Americans." I think he also wanted them to marry other Italians. But instead, they engaged in ethnic and national blending. I wonder if their spouses were "American" enough for him? Or did their choices conflict with his idea of what it is to be American? I will never know what he thought about how his family came to become multiethnic and multicultural. I do know that my mother and James Briaca's other children were more willing to make personal choices that reflected the idea of America being a "melting pot," or what I prefer to identify as a beautiful salad bowl.

MEETING THE BROWNS

At the beginning of my mother's junior year in high school, she met a lovely young African American couple, Shirley and Barfield Winslow. They moved into a small apartment building across the street from her parent's home. Agnes found them very interesting. Shirley Winslow was very pretty and tall with ash blond hair and brown eyes that were deep and piercing. She dressed in what Agnes thought of as glamorous attire. Her husband, Barfield, was very distinguished in his appearance—tall, slim, and handsome with light-brown hair, hazel eyes, and very fair skin. Their complexions were so light they could—and did—pass for White.

The couple grew up in a suburb of Hartford, Connecticut, and graduated from the University of Connecticut. They moved to Springfield to begin their careers. Barfield was a bank Manager, and Shirley worked for an insurance company. At work, their employers and colleagues assumed they were White, but their home was in an ethnically integrated neighborhood where they welcomed and entertained mostly their Black friends and family.

One day, Agnes encountered them on their street. Agnes, a very friendly and outgoing person, introduced herself to them and welcomed them to the neighborhood. They, in turn, welcomed her into their home. Shirley and Agnes were only three years apart in age and soon became close friends.

By the end of the fall of 1933, Shirley was pregnant. The baby, Beverly Marie, would be born in the early part of the following summer. Shirley and Bart asked my mother if she would babysit for them. She agreed and took care of their baby girl full-time that summer then part-time during her senior year of high school.

My mother loved little Beverly who had inherited her mother's blond hair, brown eyes, and very fair complexion. Agnes enjoyed becoming even closer to Shirley. She appreciated the trust Shirley had in her to care for her baby. She was also appreciative for the money Shirley paid her, most of which she gave to her mother to help support the family. That may be why her father didn't put her out of the family home as he had threatened to do because she was working for a Black family and had become friends with them.

Right after my mother graduated from high school in 1935, tragedy struck the young couple. Barfield had a fatal aneurysm on the floor of the bank. Following his funeral, Shirley decided to pack up her belongings and move back to Hartford, Connecticut to live at home with her parents. She realized that her parents were nearing retirement age, so she invited Agnes to move in with them to continue taking care of the baby. To sweeten the invitation, she offered to pay for Agnes to attend business/secretarial school in addition to room and board. My mother jumped at the chance to move away from her father and his threats to "put her out of the family."

Agnes was very grateful for the opportunity to earn an Associate's degree in exchange for taking care of a baby she had already grown to love. She also knew she probably wouldn't have had the opportunity for advanced education any other way.

Agnes lived with the Brown family for two years. She was a young woman who had arrived in their home like a diamond in the rough. She took pride in her appearance and practiced the best manners, but she had always aspired for more than the cultural lifestyle she experienced in her family's modest home. She was very eager to develop the graciousness that she had only seen in the movies of the 1920s and 1930s.

Shirley Winslow's parents, the Browns, had worked as servants for affluent White families for almost 50 years by the time Agnes met them. They were a well-off family with a grace and style to which my mother had never been exposed. Early in their careers, the Browns learned how to handle the finest furnishings such as imported china, sterling silverware, crystal glassware, imported table and bed linens, exquisite antiques, and handsome leather bound books. These were the types of things they chose for their own home and about which they taught Agnes.

They also taught her not to chew gum and how to set a beautiful table, and they frowned on her habit of smoking. She learned how to carry herself with grace and as Agnes would say, "how to walk, talk, and sit like a lady." It didn't seem strange to Agnes that former African American servants were teaching her the lessons she sought on manners, etiquette, and interior design. Her two-year stay with the Brown family proved to be very much like attending a finishing school, and Agnes emerged as a polished gem. She became very knowledgeable about the finer things in life as well as the rules of etiquette that reflected upper class mores and lifestyles.

It seemed to me that they smoothed out her raw edges just in time to meet my father. He had the most excellent manners and high standards of decorum thanks to his high Victorian grandmothers and aunts who raised him. So he was able to visualize her as his lifetime partner.

The finishing touches the Browns taught my mother helped my father's family to eventually accept her. My mother often quoted the Browns as she taught me these same characteristics of manners and fine living because she knew I loved and wanted to please them. In fact, during my childhood the Browns complimented her on my "manners and genteel comportment."

While growing up, I was fortunate to be able to spend time with the Browns in their lovely home. They were very kind to my mother, father, sister, and me. They also became like surrogate grandparents since my parents' parents weren't available to me. The fact that my mother met and married a Black man seemed normal to Mr. and Mrs. Brown as they saw her as a part of their family.

Mrs. Brown was an excellent cook and always made delicious meals. I loved their home because it was so large that it felt like a palace. It had many beautiful things to admire, and the atmosphere was formal and quiet.

Mr. Brown enjoyed it when we visited. We played checkers and he encouraged me to read. There was one thing about Mr. Brown that I found fascinating. He had a face full of freckles, and I don't think I had ever seen anyone else with them by then.

We visited the Browns three or four times a year usually around Christmas and Easter. The July 4th holiday was big at their house and Mr. Brown would set off fireworks in their huge backyard. Over the Labor Day weekend, we'd go to their Baptist church for a homecoming picnic where I ate my full of fried chicken and chocolate cake.

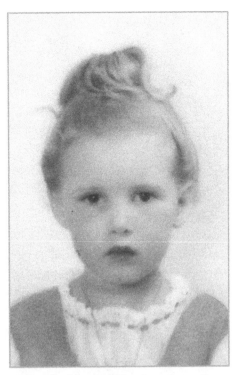

Shirley and Barfield Winslow, Agnes' new friends/employers

Beverly Marie Winslow, age 2, 1937, Hartford, CT

Shirley and June at Agnes' 60th birthday party, New Haven, CT, 1978

Agnes and Andrew on a date at Savin Rock Amusement Park, West Haven, CT, 1938

MISS AGNES E. BRAICA

Mr. and Mrs. James Braica of Orleans Street announce the engagement of their daughter, Miss Agnes E. Braica, to Andrew Murray of New Haven. The wedding date has not yet been set.

Andrew and Agnes at a dance, New Haven, CT, 1940

Agnes and Andrew celebrating Agnes' pregnancy with Cathy, New Haven, CT, 1947

Maurice and Marion Singleton (seated on floor) – Agnes and Andrew's witnesses for their wedding; in the background is Thelma Francis who became one of June's godmothers, and Agnes

Chapter Four
The Love Story

MEETING THE LOVE OF THEIR LIVES

Agnes graduated from secretarial school where she also learned bookkeeping.
She was itching to expand her horizon, and Shirley recognized it was time for
Agnes to experience more than the small suburban neighborhood outside of
Hartford, Connecticut. Also, little Beverly was ready for nursery school and
didn't need a full time nanny anymore. Agnes discussed with Shirley her
interest in moving to New York City for a while. Shirley suggested that she try
a somewhat smaller city where she could spread her wings. She offered to
connect her with a friend of her mother's who managed a small rooming
home where she could live. Agnes agreed to this plan and moved to New
Haven in April 1938.

Her landlady was an older widow with grown children who had flown
their coop. She rented out three bedrooms in a large Victorian style home in a
very nice residential neighborhood. Agnes never thought twice about
rooming with an older African American woman and two other African
American roomers, especially since the landlady was a friend of Mrs. Brown.

This was the first time in Agnes' life that she was completely out on her
own. It was also the first time she ever experienced the sting of prejudice.
Even though she was the only White person in her new community, it seemed
normal to her to live on a lovely, tree-lined street with homes owned by
working and middle-class African Americans. It reminded her of her own
street in Springfield, Massachusetts. But what was unlike her hometown
neighborhood was the distinct unfriendliness of the residents around her in

New Haven. Except for the kind and helpful woman Agnes boarded with, it was quite clear that she was not welcomed in her new neighborhood.

Agnes found a job as a bookkeeper of a large department store in Downtown, New Haven. She earned enough money to pay for her room and board, carfare, a few new clothes, and save toward the purchase of her own car. She spent her free time sitting on the front porch, watching the world around her.

By the middle of May, there was one person in particular who became of primary interest. This was the handsome young man who lived next door— Andrew Douglass Murray. She noticed he owned a stylish car and dressed in an elegant manner when he changed out of his work clothes. She assumed that he also lived in a rooming house and had a blue collar job some place. She watched as his friends came by and borrowed his car, clothes, and money. They brought back the car without gas, the clothes would be rumpled and soiled, and the money didn't seem to get returned from what she observed.

One day, she took it upon herself in her own inimitable style to speak up. Andrew was standing in front of his home after getting his car back from a friend. She called out to him and suggested he "should make his friends put some gas in the car before returning it and clean his clothes before returning them."

Curious about whom this out-spoken young woman was, Andrew walked over to her and introduced himself. He sat with her on the porch and asked how she knew so much about his personal business.

She admitted that she had been sitting on the porch watching and listening. Andrew was flattered that she was interested in his life. He inquired who she was, where she came from, and what she was doing with herself.

After that day, he would stop by most evenings to say hello. They would sit on the porch and chat about each other's day and current events. He eventually invited her to join him for rides to Savin Rock—an amusement park that was along the shore in West Haven, Connecticut. Agnes was 20 years old and was eager to see more of the city, make a new friend, and have some fun. She accepted each of his invitations for excursions around town. Gradually, she learned he didn't live in a rooming house, but owned the house he lived in as well as the house she lived in, which his aunt managed for him. She also learned that while it was true that he was a blue-collar worker, he owned the printing business where he worked.

Andrew began to introduce her to some of his friends. He took her to affairs in the African American community such as dances, cookouts, and house parties. My mother shared that while those affairs were fun, they provoked extreme anxiety. My father's friends, more so his female friends, made it clear they didn't welcome her because she was White and wasn't from New Haven. They felt she was an intrusion into their social lives and showed no warmth or friendliness towards her. I learned about the bias my mother experienced during my teens when I shared with her similar resentment I was encountering at African American social events in New Haven. Some of the girls expressed their bias about my skin color and my hair texture. They also considered me an "outsider" as my mother had been viewed because when I was six years old my family moved to Milford, where I attended high school.

In 1938—even in Connecticut—Black men didn't openly date White women, but Andrew was 35 years old and felt independent. He realized that he was attracted to this stylish, young woman who was his new neighbor. She was outspoken and direct, and he liked her exuberance. After all, Agnes was young and she naturally wanted to have some fun. He could see that she was not a gold digger, and he liked that she seemed to care about him. She gave him advice about saving his money and showed concern about how others treated him.

Agnes was the first person in Andrew's life after his mother died that made him feel as though he was worthwhile. Both sets of his grandparents cared for him and his brother Douglass, but the family's grief over the loss of their mother was so great that the boys were emotionally neglected. Agnes was eager for his company and appreciated his sense of humor. Her caring response led him to fall head over heels in love with her.

For Agnes, except for the men in her friend Shirley's family, Andrew was the first man who treated her with respect. He was raised with Victorian gentility and ultra conservative manners, so he was always a gentleman. He was soft-spoken, gentle, and very sensitive in an intuitive manner. Agnes could feel his concern for her welfare and appreciated his attention. She, too, fell very much in love.

I would like to say that Andrew's friends supported his decision to ask Agnes to marry him, but the truth is they were (certainly the females) adamantly against their friendship and potential marriage. They used the stereotypes commonly accepted among Black communities about "White, low-life women" to try to dissuade Andrew from marrying Agnes. They played tricks to try to prove she was unfaithful. Lies were told, arguments ensued, and they warned him that marriages between Blacks and Whites didn't work out. But Andrew was a good judge of character, and he loved and trusted Agnes. He met her friend Shirley and her parents and saw how much they loved and accepted her as a "daughter." He knew about Agnes' family of origin, her quest for an education, and that she was a hard worker. She earned Andrew's trust and always lived up to it.

Andrew and Agnes were not deterred by the racism of the day. By July of 1938, they felt their love was solid. In August, Andrew proposed. They went to the Minister at St. Luke's and requested to be married in the church, but the Minister refused. He explained that the congregation of the church including my father's family would oppose the marriage because they were a bi-ethnic couple. The minister also felt it would cause a great deal of trouble for him if he approved their marriage and performed the ceremony.

An Associate Minister, Rev. John Edwards of Jamaica, West Indies, overheard their conversation and later approached my father. He invited the couple to meet with him at the church. He counseled the young couple and found sincerity in their hearts. He knew they had been baptized/christened in the eyes of God and believed they should be married in the church. Rev. Edwards agreed to perform the ceremony if Andrew and Agnes brought two witnesses and came to the church on a Wednesday night when the lead Minister wouldn't be there.

My father asked Maurice and Marion Singleton, one of his best friends since childhood and his wife, to serve as his Best Man and Matron of Honor. On October 7, 1938, they were joined in holy matrimony in a simple but significant ceremony at St. Luke's—the same church Andrew's family helped to build.

The lead minister was correct in his opinion that the church congregation would oppose this marriage. My father's family created quite a stir and complained to him for many years about his choice to marry a White woman. Many in the family also looked down on her due to her economic background.

Only one of Andrew's aunts, his father's sister Daisy, supported his decision. Another aunt, his mother's sister Jane, grew to appreciate my mother's devotion to my father. His friends eventually became fond of Agnes and some of them later became my godparents. And, as is typical in the

African American Village model, these friends helped guide my growth as well as my sister's well into our adulthood.

As one would expect in any marriage, my parents had their ups and downs. The downs weren't related to their different ethnicities as their friends predicted, but had more to do with their personalities. My mother often told me a cute story about a situation that took place soon after they got married. As the story goes, she cooked my father's favorite vegetable—lima beans. She greeted him when he came home from work that evening and she said, "Dinner is ready, but let me go and change first." When she returned to the kitchen, she found my father on his hands and knees. He seemed to be shooting something like a marble on the floor—it was one of her lima beans.

At this point in the story, Dad would chime in while smiling that famous smile of his and say, "But those beans were hard as marbles."

I understand there were a lot of tears that night and extensive apologies. Over the years, my mother never saw the humor in his response to her lima beans. However, she did learn how to make lima beans and never let my father forget that! Daddy would smile at the dinner table and say, "Please pass those delicious lima beans," then smiled his cute devilish grin at my mother.

Some of the downs in their marriage resulted from my mother's few unsmoothed edges. She cursed which made my father just about faint. She was always outspoken and valiant in her defense of her family, especially when anyone exhibited racial bias against us. Agnes was a warrior when it came to making sure that we were treated fairly, respectfully, and courteously. People didn't make the mistake of racially insulting us more than once. I am certain this behavior is another aspect of my mother's personality that I "inherited."

I love to tell about an experience we often had, which I call the "family parade." We ate out in restaurants quite often. My father, the perfect gentleman at all times, would drive up to the restaurant door to let my mother out of the car before parking. I always wanted to get out with her, and my sister usually wanted to stay in the car with him. My mother would walk into the restaurant with me close behind her. When the maître d's asked her "how many," she would tell them four and that her husband and other daughter was parking the car. They would smile and sort of glance at me. Soon, my sister would walk in. Now, she must have inherited her great grandmother's Native American genes, as her skin color is close to the color of walnuts. The maître d's would give her a longer glance, but not pay too much attention to her. Right behind her would be my father and there was no question about his ethnicity. At that point, the air around the maître d's became cooler. Still they would grab some menus and inform us to follow them. They would start wending their way through the restaurant to a table in the back of the room next to the exit sign, kitchen door, or the restroom.

My father, sister, and I would follow my mother to the table the maître d' selected then my mother would say, "Thank you, but this won't do. We'd like that table in the front of the restaurant in the window." She would turn on her heels and lead the family like a parade back through the restaurant to a front table with an air of confidence and defiance. If the maître d's tuned up their lips to complain, the look my mother gave them changed their minds immediately. My father would follow in his place in the parade without comment, hold the chairs at the preferred table for his wife and his daughters, then sit down and begin to peruse the menu. I loved the family parade. If you ever go to a restaurant with me and the waitress takes me to a table near the bathroom, backdoor, or kitchen, you can bet your last dollar we will be on a parade right back through the restaurant.

Despite the chastisement they initially experienced from my father's friends, the threats of being disowned from their families, and the hostility and overt expressions of racism they encountered in city restaurants, movie theaters, church, and various stores, they were blessed with a love and marriage that lasted for 53 years until my father's transition.

Murrays married 49 years

Mr. and Mrs. Andrew Murray celebrated their forty-ninth wedding anniversary in festivities at Pond Point Health Care Center, 60 Platt St.

The Rev. David Angelica of St. Andrew's Episcopal renewed their wedding vows.

The couple was married October 7, 1938 in New Haven.

Mr. and Mrs. Andrew Murray

Andrew and Agnes enjoying a dance, New Haven, CT, 1970s

Andrew and Agnes at Agnes' 60th birthday party, New Haven, CT, 1978

Agnes and Andrew celebrating their 50th Wedding Anniversary with June and her daughter Robin, Milford, CT, 1988

June and her baby sister Cathy, godparents Rudy (sunglasses) and Thelma Francis (holding baby), June on godmother, Elsie Harris', lap, Pete Harris, and Andrew in the background, Cape Cod, MA, 1949

Andrew's Uncle Charlie and Aunt Corrine Murray who advised them to adopt as they had done, New Bedford, MA

Chapter Five
One then Two, and Baby Makes Three

It was fascinating for me to have the opportunity to hear about what happened next from my mother and birthmother. This is one of the chapters in my adoption story that is almost identical except for one fact. There are several other incidents in the story that have slightly different versions, depending on whether it is Agnes or Shirley who is relating the memory. But what happened next seems to have been as follows.

My parents worried that they might not be able to have children because many of the women in my father's family had difficulty conceiving. They didn't know why this was true. They only knew that very few children were born to the women on both sides of my father's family. My parents were very progressive so they discussed the possibility of adopting if they were not blessed with a pregnancy. Around the tenth month of their marriage, my mother experienced a miscarriage in her third week of pregnancy. The doctor told her she was fine and to try again, but years went by without another pregnancy.

In 1941, my parents went to see my father's uncle Charlie and aunt Corinne in New Bedford, Massachusetts. They had adopted a daughter, Mary Corinne, in 1930 who was eleven years old at the time of the meeting. Agnes and Andrew wanted to know what the process was like to adopt a child and how the Murray family accepted their decision to adopt. They were curious about what it was like being adoptive parents. They wanted to learn about the rules governing private adoptions, which was legal in Connecticut at that time. However, Agnes and Andrew's primary concern was whether the

State adoption agency would allow them to adopt since they were an interracial couple.

THE KEY PEOPLE THEY MET

In January of 1942, my mother accepted a bookkeeping job with the Winchester Rifle Factory. The company had become a defense plant for the U.S. Department of Defense during World War II. She got to know some of the employees and became friends with one young woman in particular. Her name was Shirley O'Mara who coincidentally had the same first name as my mother's good friend, Shirley Winslow.

Shirley was 20 years old and a member of the fifth generation of an Irish-American, Catholic family. Agnes described her as very spunky with a great voice. She loved to sing and entertain her colleagues very much like the scenes from WWII movies when someone would jump up on a table and belt out a patriotic song. Agnes thought she was a nice person, and they often shared their lunch period chatting, gossiping, and passing the time together.

Agnes' office was in the loft of the factory so from her vantage point, she could see the employees working on the assembly line on the main floor. She noticed a handsome, charismatic, young African American man by the name of Louis Barclay. He came to town to work at the defense plant where he could earn a very good living. The defense plant hired many women who were supporting their families while their husbands were away at war. Louis' female coworkers—Black and White—found him irresistible. He seemed more than happy to spend some quality time with them. As Agnes put it, he worked his way up one side and down the other of the assembly lines, encountering very little resistance to his charm.

Agnes discussed this situation with Andrew. She suggested that sooner or later a child might come from such passionate dedication. She also thought the child might come at an inconvenient time or to someone who was unable to accommodate such a surprise. She then asked Andrew if they should consider adopting such a child.

Andrew was as eager to have a family as Agnes was, so he made some inquiries around the community about Louis. He learned that Louis wasn't married (at least he didn't have a wife in New Haven), lived alone in a rooming house, and men around town didn't like him very much. Some of the negative reaction to Louis was because he was six feet, five inches tall, very handsome, a great debater, a good poker player, somewhat argumentative, and rather arrogant. He had a way with women that some local men, according to my father's observations, may have resented. On top of that, he claimed to be from New York City and had a "city slicker" air about him that annoyed local New Haven males. So they decided he wasn't to be trusted. That was the general rule of the Black and "closed" New Haven society. African Americans in New Haven were very provincial about who was a true "New Havener" and who wasn't. Many people in the community were very unwelcoming to newcomers.

Through Agnes' interactions with Louis on paydays, she observed that he was quite smart. She thought he could've had a successful professional career if he had been afforded a better education. She didn't like his personality but saw he was healthy, didn't appear to be a drinker, and had very good discipline. He never had problems with tardiness, absenteeism, or conflicts on the job with his supervisor or colleagues. She felt these characteristics and aspects of his personality were important as the possible father of her future child.

She and Andrew agreed that if a child came from a union between Louis and one of the women at the plant and the child was available for adoption, they would seek to adopt that child.

One day Shirley told Agnes that Louis had invited her to go out with him. Agnes warned her to be careful and reminded her that Louis tended to be rather arrogant to put it mildly. He also didn't usually date any one woman more than once or twice. Later, Agnes told me that she had a premonition that a child would come from the union between Shirley and Louis.

Shirley had one date with Louis, and it pleased her that he behaved like a gentleman. A week or so later, she accepted a second invitation for a date during which Shirley succumbed to Louis' charms. Apparently, there were no further dates between them.

In early October of 1942, Shirley asked Agnes to meet with her after work. She had a long face and didn't display her usual happy-go-lucky demeanor. Agnes told me their conversation went like this:

"Agnes, I have a problem—"

"I know. You're pregnant!"

"How did you know?"

"I've been watching you and Louis…he's the father, right?"

"Yes, and you know I can't keep this baby!"

"Does Louis know?"

"Yes, I told him last night, and he took me to the drug store and bought me some sort of powder that he told me it would either bring on my period or make sure I remained pregnant. Then he told me I was on my own!"

"I see. So, how can I help you?"

"Well, I know you are married to a Colored fellow, and I was thinking you don't have any children, and this baby will be just like what you and Andy would have. And, well, maybe you might consider adopting it."

"Well, Andrew and I have discussed this possibility and we would be interested as long as you agreed to our terms."

"Terms? What would they be?"

"You allow us to select the OB/GYN. We'll pay for him and all of your prenatal care and we would select the hospital, and you would not smoke or drink alcohol during your pregnancy. If the baby is healthy at birth, we will adopt it. And we will select and pay for an attorney to take care of all the legal arrangements, and you will sign away all rights to the baby so you don't change your mind later on."

"You know I can't bring a Colored baby home to my family. Just being pregnant and not being married is bad enough…but a Colored baby? My family will never forgive me. My father will put me out of his home!"

Shirley had already decided to give up her child for adoption. In 1942, unmarried women didn't strike out on their own with a child, especially if they were White with a bi-racial child. Furthermore, Shirley was still living at home with her parents and couldn't sustain herself financially let alone provide for a child. Abortion was out of the question because she was raised in the Catholic faith. She had the choice to either leave the baby at an orphanage or to place the baby with a loving family. I am eternally grateful for the choice she made.

Later that month Shirley married a Jewish man named Sidney Cushen, who was very much in love with her. He married her knowing she was pregnant and promised to raise the child she was carrying as though it was his own.

When Shirley and I talked about this period of our lives, she shared that her parents weren't pleased she was dating a Russian man of the Jewish faith. Even during World War II when most eligible men were away fighting in the war, Shirley's parents' response to any non-Catholic, non-Irish suitor for their daughter's hand was negative. But Shirley didn't let their issues stop her from accepting Louis Barclay's invitation for a date or Sidney Cushen's marriage proposal. Shirley was glad to get married so she could conceal her pregnancy from her parents, siblings, and friends for a while. When it became obvious that she was pregnant, people assumed the baby was her husband's child even if they thought she conceived it before her marital bonds.

Shirley O'Mara Cushen and her brother Bill O'Mara in her early stage of pregnancy with June, New Haven, CA, 1942

June's godparents, Elsie and Pete Harris, with her parents, New Haven, CA, 1970's

Chapter Six
The Adoption Unfolds

Agnes and Andrew agreed to adopt Shirley's child. They informed Shirley they would adopt the baby if it was born healthy, but they would cancel the plan if the baby was not in good health. Years later, when Agnes and Andrew told me about the planning that went into the adoption, they emphatically stated they would've adopted me if I had been born with two heads.

My soon-to-be parents developed a very elaborate plan for the adoption. They located an obstetrician/gynecologist, Dr. Louis Gentile, for Shirley's prenatal care and chose New Haven Hospital for the birth. They made all the arrangements and payments for Shirley's OB/GYN's visits throughout the next seven months of her pregnancy. They purchased Shirley's maternity clothing and secured a private room for when she was ready to deliver her baby.

Agnes and Andrew engaged an attorney, Elliot Goldman, to ensure that they could indeed legally adopt the child she was carrying. This was a major concern because Shirley had married Sidney during the second month of her pregnancy. They needed an attorney who could investigate the laws pertaining to a couple surrendering their child as well as the laws concerning private adoptions in Connecticut. The attorney handled all the legal details of the adoption including whether Agnes and Andrew could have custody of the baby upon discharge from the hospital.

Dr. Gentile agreed to cooperate fully with Agnes, Andrew, and Shirley with regard to the logistics of the adoption. He instructed the nursing staff to not provide any information to anyone who might inquire about the new infant born to Shirley Cushen. Their script was, "The mother is fine, no comment on the baby." The attorney was also very supportive of Agnes and Andrew's plans. The physician and the attorney praised them and Shirley for making such careful plans to safeguard the wellbeing and privacy of the baby.

Only my parents' closest friends knew they were about to adopt, but they didn't know who the birthmother was nor did they ask. By this time, Agnes was well received into the closely knit circle of my father's friends, having proven herself as his best ally. His friends loved her and appreciated how happy she had made him. So they were looking forward to the blessed event as much as the soon-to-be parents.

Agnes and Andrew continued to prepare for my birth. They beautifully decked out my nursery with lots of pastel-pink and blue fairytale designs. Curtains draped over the windows and they bought a bassinet, bathinette, and carriage. Agnes and her close friends knitted tons of sweaters, bonnets, and blankets. They bought toys, cloth diapers, and everything anyone could think of to welcome the Murray baby. Meanwhile, Shirley's family held a baby shower for her and also made sure her baby would have the necessary things she would need.

The only task Agnes and Andrew left to Shirley was to inform her husband, and then their families of their decision to allow another couple to adopt their baby. It was left up to them to explain why they chose adoption. It is important to note Shirley's baby could not be adopted unless both legal parents signed the official documentation agreeing to this plan, and I was legally Sidney's child at birth.

THE PLOT THICKENS

On Saturday morning, June 19, 1943, Agnes and Andrew received a telephone call from their dearest friends, Pete and Elsie Harris. Andrew knew this couple since the age of six when they began elementary school together. Pete and Elsie were the first to recover from the shock of Andrew marrying an Italian, non-New Havener woman and to welcome her into their tightly knit circle of friends. That morning the Harris' called to invite Agnes and Andrew to join them for dinner to celebrate Father's Day. Agnes inquired if Elsie needed them to bring anything, and Elsie asked if they could stop at the corner market and pick up an item.

Later that day around 4:00 p.m. as Agnes and Andrew were walking through the market, Agnes suddenly doubled over with abdominal pain. She felt nauseous and dizzy then she passed out. Andrew carried her to their car. They were closer to the Harris' home than their own so he drove her there and stretched her out on their sofa. Pete was a biochemist so he examined Agnes. He concluded that she was struck with a 24-hour grip and believed she would be fine soon.

The dinner party went on with several other friends. They all watched over Agnes as she periodically felt dizzy, nauseous, and experienced pain in her abdominal area. She had sweats, no appetite, and was miserable. By 5:00 a.m. the next morning, she fell into a peaceful sleep. Everyone decided the grip had passed through her, and she would be fine as Pete predicted. The Harris' and Andrew went to bed as the other guests had long since departed.

Agnes got up around 8:00 a.m. to the smell of bacon frying and the sound of eggs cracking into a bowl. She woke up Andrew and asked him to go to their home to get her a fresh change of clothing. In his calm and peaceful style, Andrew drove home to collect the items his wife asked for and to freshen up. The phone was ringing as he walked into the house. It was Dr. Gentile, and Andrew said the conversation went something like this:

"Andrew? Where the hell have you been? I've been calling you since just after 5:00 this morning!"

"Oh, well, we were out celebrating Father's Day."

"What? Well…how did you know?"

"How did I know what?"

"That you're a father! Congratulations! Shirley had the baby at 5 a.m. this morning! She was in labor since yesterday afternoon from around 4 p.m., but she's fine. Come on down and see your baby!"

Agnes didn't have the 24-hour grip after all, but had experienced sympathy labor pains. Andrew, known for his methodical-ism showered, dressed, packed up some clothes for Agnes then drove back to the Harris' home.

When he walked in, Agnes greeted him in her usual volatile manner, "Where in the world have you been? I'm starving, but I can't come to the breakfast table in Pete's bathrobe. And I've been waiting for you. What took so long?"

"Well, I had to shower and change too, you know, and anyway we had a telephone call," Andrew calmly answered.

At this point, everyone got very quiet—Elsie stopped cooking, Pete stopped fussing with the newspaper, and they focused their attention on Andrew.

Agnes asked, "A phone call? Who called at this hour in the morning?"

Andrew still calm as usual answered, "Dr. Gentile…it seems there's been a baby born. We are now parents!"

At that point, pandemonium broke loose! Everyone looked like the Keystone Kops running around bumping into each other. They were rushing around getting their clothes and shoes on, picking up their keys, and turning off the stove.

Elsie suddenly stopped. "Is it a girl or boy?" she asked Andrew.

"Oh, I don't know, Dr. Gentile didn't say," Andrew answered in his typical low-key manner.

The four of them rushed out of the door and drove together to the hospital. They went to the nursery window and searched for the Cushen baby. Three African Americans and one White woman with their faces pressed against the window took the nurse by surprise. Dr. Gentile had informed the nursing staff that no information should be given about the Cushen baby, but he didn't informed them that the baby was bi-ethnic. So the nurse had no idea who the guests were looking for. She walked out of the nursery into the hallway and asked if she could be of assistance. When they told her who they were looking for, she pointed to the baby bed in front of the nursery right under their noses. The reason the group couldn't find the newborn they came to visit was because they were looking for a baby with a bit more hue. Instead, I was all peaches and cream in complexion, wrapped up in a pink blanket and dreaming my new baby dreams.

Agnes left the group and went to find Shirley's room. She found Shirley in a complete state of panic, and she told Agnes everything that happened earlier that morning. Shirley said she was too afraid to tell Sidney she had become pregnant by an African American or as they called us in those days—"Colored." She also never told him of her plan to give the baby up for adoption. So during labor and after her baby was born, she was worried about her husband's reaction when he saw their child. She too expected the baby to be a darker hue.

Shirley had not seen me following my birth because the nurses had whisked me away to care for me in the nursery per her request. One can imagine how confusing it was for Sidney when Dr. Gentile came from the delivery room and told him he could see his wife, but there was "no comment" about the baby. The situation became even more difficult for Sidney when he asked Shirley about their baby and Shirley informed him that their baby had died.

Sidney was an Orthodox Jew and while he couldn't understand why or how the baby had died, he told Shirley that they had to sit Shiva for the child. He asked her where the baby's body was because he didn't think the hospital would dispose of the corpse. Shirley couldn't talk to him about the situation or bring herself to explain the truth. All she could do was cry.

Sidney took matters into his own hands. He went back to the nursery and demanded to see his child. The nurses were in a panic and refused to discuss the matter with Sidney. They told him to ask his wife about the baby but instead, Sidney burst into the nursery. He looked at all the baby's wrist for a beaded bracelet with his name on it, and he found me. He picked me up and asked the nurse why his wife told him that I had died. The nurses had no idea Shirley told him such a story, so they reiterated that he had to ask his wife. The nurse took me from him and returned me to my little bed.

Sidney returned to Shirley's room and demanded an explanation. He told her that he had seen me and I was most definitely not dead.

Shirley blurted out, "If you saw the baby then you know why I said it had died!"

Sidney still didn't understand what in the world was going on.

"Didn't you see what the baby looks like?" Shirley asked.

"Yes," Sidney responded, "she looks like she could be my baby, but I know that isn't possible."

Shirley didn't understand how looking at me didn't tell Sidney about my ethnicity, but then she said, "Well, I don't know what she looks like now, but any minute she will be as black as the ace of spades." At that point, she went on to explain that my biological father was "Colored" and she made arrangements with a "bi-racially" married couple to adopt me.

As Sidney listened to Shirley's explanation and her plans for me, he became furious. I don't know if he was angrier because his wife had joined in union with a Black man, or that she made arrangements for his child to be adopted without his input. All I know is he left the hospital and told Shirley he didn't want to speak to her.

Shirley discussed that morning with me many years later. I shared with her what Agnes told me about that day, especially her interaction with her husband. She agreed with everything Agnes told me, but she denied making the comment about the "Ace of Spades." As I got to know her and listened to her explanation about why she couldn't have kept me, I think Agnes had it right. I think Shirley did believe I would darken in complexion and there would be no doubt about my ethnicity. Therefore, there was no way she could've brought me home to the O'Mara family whom she described as extremely racist. She also shared that her husband's parents were unhappy their son married out of their faith so bringing home a "Colored" baby would've probably ended any relationship she had with them.

Shirley apologized to Agnes after telling her about her husband's reaction. She was afraid that Sidney would leave her and not sign the legal documents allowing my adoption to proceed. After all, legally I was his child and the adoption couldn't occur without his approval. He could have decided to place me in an orphanage.

Agnes and Andrew went home and called Sidney. They begged him to visit them so they could explain their interest in adopting his child. Sidney agreed to visit them the next day.

Agnes and Andrew saw that he was quite amazed when he walked into their home. By then, they had purchased a three family house in a lovely neighborhood. They rented out the first and third floors and lived on the second floor. Their home was filled with elegant furnishings, and Agnes showed him the nursery they had decked out.

Sidney had trouble making ends meet, and it was obvious that Agnes and Andrew could provide the child with far more than he could. Agnes and Andrew also believed that when Sidney saw they were a bi-ethnic couple, he understood why Shirley selected them as the adoptive parents of her child. Before leaving their home, he agreed to the adoption and signed the legal documents allowing it to move forward.

Shirley and Sidney agreed to tell their families that the baby was stillborn. It's not clear what they said happened to the baby following the birth, but there weren't any questions concerning a funeral from anyone in either family. So no one in their families saw me or knew I continued to exist following my birth.

Agnes and Andrew's families of origin knew I had been adopted, but they didn't know where I came from or who my birthparents were. Agnes' family's reaction to her marriage to a "Colored" man stood in the way of any sort of bonding process her father or siblings might have pursued. Her mother had to sneak away from her home to see me during the first few weeks of my life.

In order to finalize the adoption in Connecticut, the adoption had to be posted in a daily circulating newspaper for seven consecutive days. The listing had to specify the names of the birthparents, the adopted parents, and the date of birth of the adopted child. Agnes, ever clever and wise, found a Danish-language newspaper published in a New Haven neighborhood where there was a meat packing business that primarily employed people from Denmark. The State of Connecticut law didn't state the newspaper had to be printed in English. So from June 22nd through June 29th, there was one little item printed in English in that newspaper. Hence, the busybodies of New Haven never learned where the new Murray baby came from. My adoption became final six weeks following my birth. It was the last private adoption to occur in the State of Connecticut for over 30 years.

My mother cut that announcement out of the newspaper and placed it in a book on the bookshelf for safekeeping. It was that newspaper clipping my sister found thirteen years later, which started my journey towards accepting my adoption.

– # –

Six weeks after I was born, Agnes' father died suddenly and she took me with her to his funeral. After the burial, everyone returned to her mother's house including my mother and me. As the family members gathered in the backyard garden with some refreshments, my mother placed me in my carriage with a gauze mosquito net over it. She noticed her sisters and other family members trying to sneak a peek at me through the net. So she walked over to them and asked if they would like to see her baby daughter and they nodded. She removed the net and lifted me up. Agnes said, "They just stared in what seemed like amazement." Probably, like Shirley, they expected something quite different with regard to my skin color and hair. Her godmother Agatha was the first to recover her composure, and she praised Agnes for such a beautiful baby.

My mother took great pleasure in sharing this encounter with me, but there were other memories that were painful to talk about like the first time Shirley and I met.

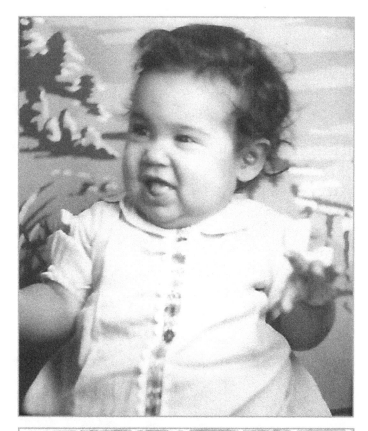

June at
6 months

Agnes and
Andrew with
one year old
June, 1944

CHAPTER SEVEN
Remembering a Special Heartbeat

It's clear that Agnes and Shirley were quite progressive for their era. One married outside her ethnic group and was eager to adopt a bi-ethnic child while the other dated and married outside her ethnic and religious group.

As these women journeyed through Shirley's pregnancy, they made many plans from Shirley's prenatal care to the legal aspects of the adoption. They plotted and schemed to protect the identity and privacy of the infant as well as the parents. They daydreamed about how their little baby would learn about his/her adoption. The women also thought about how to make sure the child never doubted that he/she was loved by all concerned.

One plan they labored over throughout the pregnancy turned out to be far more difficult to execute than they thought. The plan centered around their wish to remain close friends, and it included the idea that Shirley would often visit Agnes and Andrew and their child. They wanted the child to grow up knowing Shirley as a close family friend and over time, he or she would somehow glean the knowledge that Shirley was actually his or her birthmother. That was a pretty progressive manner of thinking, and an idea with the highest intentions for the security and nurturance of the expected newcomer.

Once Agnes and Andrew brought me home from the hospital, Shirley found it difficult to visit. Agnes and Shirley spoke quite frequently on the telephone, but she was unable to travel the short distance to the Murray home. Shirley promised again and again to come over to see the baby and to bring the gifts she received at her baby shower, but months passed by without a visit.

As the Christmas holiday of 1943 approached and I was reaching six months of age, Shirley forced herself to visit. She brought with her the only shower gift I hadn't outgrown—a clear Lucite brush, comb, and mirror set (incidentally, I still own the mirror). Agnes greeted Shirley while holding me in her arms, and she invited her to have a seat. Once Shirley was settled in the chair, Agnes very magnanimously placed me on her lap. Agnes said I enjoyed this interaction as I was a very outgoing baby, and I seemed to like playing with Shirley's earrings and necklace.

After Agnes and Shirley chatted for a while, I began to get sleepy and placed my head on Shirley's upper chest. This intimate gesture was very alarming to Agnes and Shirley. Agnes stood up and told Shirley it was my nap time and she should take me to my room so I could sleep in my crib. Shirley agreed and started to hand me to Agnes. As she reached for me, I pulled back and clung to Shirley's neck. Shirley tried to pry my little hands loose while Agnes tried to pull me into her arms. I shrieked. Shirley began to cry and so did Agnes.

I've been told that normally I was eager to go into my mother's arms, but not this time. Eventually, Agnes got a secure hold of me. She carried me out of the room and walked towards my bedroom. I cried all the way down the hall. Even after Agnes placed me into the crib, my shrieks could be heard throughout the house. It wasn't until more than fifty years had passed that Shirley and I laid eyes on one another again.

I was 20 years old when I first heard about this visit from my mother. It was a few months after the birth of my first child when we had the discussion. Agnes began to tear up as she related her memories of what happened. She explained that it was obvious to her and Shirley that I knew it was my biological mother holding me. But I scoffed at her belief. I told her I was probably spoiled and enjoyed the company of a new face. Or maybe I liked the feel and sound of Shirley's jewelry. Then I reminded her I always liked to be held. I told her another possibility was that I didn't want to take a nap. Agnes disagreed and insisted it was very clear to her and Shirley that I knew or sensed whom Shirley was. She went on to say that nothing would ever convince her otherwise.

Thirty years later, Shirley shared this exact story with me. It amazed me that she came to the same conclusion as Agnes. She was convinced I knew who was holding me. She believed I had some sort of primal instinct and could identify her body scent, voice, and heartbeat. I scoffed at her too and told her the same thing that I told Agnes. I was convinced I had no way of knowing who was holding me, and that it was an emotional experience for the three of us for different reasons. They had their knowledge of who was who in my life, and I believed that made them think I also knew.

Three years after Shirley told me this same story about her one and only visit to the Murray household, I witnessed my grandson Christopher being delivered into this world. When he was only minutes old, I saw how he reacted to the voices of his mother, father, and mine. He quieted down at the sound of our voices, particularly when his mother held him. When she spoke, he turned his head so he could look into her face. He also turned his head towards his father and me when we were talking.

It was clear he knew us and was able to screen out the doctor's voice, as well as the voices of the nurses who were caring for him. At that moment, I realized Agnes and Shirley were right. I did know Shirley and did remember her voice, her scent, and the feel and sound of her heartbeat.

That was such a traumatic experience for those two women that they never planned any further visits, but they did remain in touch with each other. Agnes kept Shirley updated on my growth and progress from my infancy well into my middle-age adulthood. In fact, Agnes and Shirley would talk and catch each other up on their families for the next fifty years. The only reason that communication stopped was because of my mother's final stroke that prohibited her from speaking.

June at age one on a visit to Agnes' family of origin, Springfield, MA, 1944

June at 4 years and 10 months old just before she left for Alabama in her home's rose garden with family friends, the Williams', New Haven, CT, 1948

June in backyard with Andrew, May 1948, one month before her trip to Alabama

Chapter Eight
A Mysterious Decision – Was I Being Sent Away?

When I was two years old, my mother pushed me in my stroller to the neighborhood pharmacy. I fell asleep so she parked the stroller in front of the plate glass window and went inside to purchase an item from the cashier at the front of the store. She could see me from where she was standing inside the store. An older woman came along on the sidewalk, unlocked the brakes on the stroller, and started pushing me away. My mother ran outside and rescued me. The old woman said she was "taking my grandchild home," which led my mother to believe she had some sort of dementia.

My parents had always been protective of me but after that experience, they never left me alone or with any of their close friends for more than two hours. Instead of using babysitters, they took me just about everywhere they went. My mother was an at-home mom but when she let me go to nursery school at age three, it was only for two hours each morning.

Their friends were my father's age, which was fifteen years older than my mother. They married young so their children were much older, and most had already left home for college or entered the military. Therefore, I was the only child around. I have to say I was cute and precocious, but very well mannered. I really loved attention, which I received from everyone in my life. My parents were always welcome to bring me along with them to visits in their friends' homes. When it was time for me to go to sleep, I would be placed on a friend's bed surrounded by pillows. The adults in my parents' social circle watched over and entertained me, and seemed to take great delight in my company. My parents' friends were my "Aunties and Uncles" in the fictive kin/extended family norm so common in Black communities of that era, and these wonderful friends formed our "village."

Four months after I turned four years old, my parents learned they were about to have a baby. I was excited about this news because I wanted a baby brother or sister. So life up to this point was like a beautiful dream. Then one day in April of 1948 when I was almost five years old, my parents took me to visit some of their friends. There was a young woman by the name of Maude in the group who was visiting New Haven for the first time. She came with one of my father's male childhood friends. Although he was from New Haven, he relocated to New York City once he returned from his military service in World War II. He and Maude met in New York City, and he brought her home to meet his family and friends.

During the visit, Maude overheard one of my "aunties" ask my mother what she planned to do with me when the baby comes while she would be hospitalized? My mother told my auntie that she didn't know. In those days, women stayed in the hospital following childbirth for at least a week. My parents' friends were employed so they couldn't take care of me for that long. Everyone knew that the family members on both sides of my family weren't available to care for me because of their bias or age. Also, my father still owned his printing business and needed to be in his shop.

The young woman from New York City spoke up and offered to take me with her to visit her parents in Alabama. She said her "parents had just moved into a new farmhouse," and they had "lots of land where I could play." She added she had "younger brothers who would enjoy my visit." While she was speaking, I was sitting on her lap and playing with her jewelry. I found her interesting because she was a newcomer to the social circle and I liked the diversion.

I can only assume that my parents had additional discussions with Maude that I was not privy to. All I know is that one day in mid-June I was taken to New York City's Grand Central Station by my father who was carrying my new little pink suitcase, and Maude met us at the train station. I barely remembered the young woman whom I had met two months earlier. My father told me I was to spend two weeks with Maude at her parents' home in Alabama, but I was too young to understand what two weeks meant or what Alabama was. Then all of a sudden my father was gone and I was left with Maude.

Years later, I was told that my father gave Maude two round-trip tickets for a compartment car with beds and a tiny bathroom. Once my father left us at the station, Maude returned those tickets and bought one-way tickets for a coach seat. For one thing, she knew that in 1948 Black people couldn't travel in compartment cars below Washington, D.C. It would seem to me that my father and mother knew that as well because many of my father's friends were Pullman Porters, and they shared many stories of their experiences on the trains. More importantly though, my parents learned that Maude was struggling financially, and her intention was to pocket the extra money she received from turning in the more expensive tickets.

In the beginning, the train ride with Maude was fun. She allowed me to walk up and down the aisle and make "friends" with the other passengers. When I tired of those activities, I sat on Maude's lap or next to her if there was an available seat. After a long day of an often crowded train ride, traipsing up and down the aisle and eating sandwiches from the bar car (Blacks weren't served in the dining car), I fell asleep.

I woke up in the middle of the night only to notice that Maude wasn't sitting near me nor was she in the train car. Then I realized that my new "friends" were also missing (having gotten off at their destinations while I slept). You can imagine what it was like for a child who is not quite five years old to be on a moving train, in the dark, surrounded by strangers, without her parents for the first time in her life, and the one person she had to rely on was gone.

Another passenger noticed that I was awake and probably frightened. That passenger went to the bar car where Maude was enjoying herself and told her that her "daughter" was awake. Maude returned to her seat and I suppose comforted me to some degree. Later, Maude told my parents that I didn't cry out or move from my seat. I guess the stoicism that characterized New Englanders was already instilled in me.

The next morning we arrived in a small town in Alabama. We then made a long journey to Maude's parents' farm, which was located in a rural section of the state. I do remember that Maude's mother and father were not at all pleased that she had brought me with her. They were concerned about who I was, why she had me with her, and if the law might be looking for me. They also weren't sure what my ethnicity was, which made them even more nervous. To say they were cold towards me would be an understatement—that much I do remember. And her "younger brothers" who worked on their farm, turned out to be between 18 and 20 years of age.

The farmhouse was new, but it didn't have porch stairs yet, and the first story was about four feet off the ground. At this point in my life, I was not quite three feet tall so I couldn't get into or out of the house without help. So at 4 A.M. when it was still pitch-black outside, Maude's brothers would wake me up before they left for work and ask, "In or out?" I would have to decide at that moment if I wanted to be outside or inside all day. It was their job to lift me off the mattress and put me outside on the ground for the day if I chose *out*. I must add that whether I was *in* or *out*, the heat was stifling all day and through the nights.

Maude would bring me breakfast and lunch outside if that was where I was, and she would feed me dinner inside later in the day. I don't remember much about the food. However, there wasn't any electricity yet, so the milk they gave me came straight from the cow and it was hot and disgusting.

My little corner in the house consisted of a mattress on the floor without linens or a bed frame. It was near the doorway, which had no door and was supposed to be the cooler part of the house. It was also an easy access for all types of creatures.

I had nothing to do on the farm. There weren't any children around or toys, except the few my parents packed in my suitcase. There also wasn't any indoor plumbing and being a city child, you can imagine how traumatic it was for me to use an outhouse—the stench, flies, and the possibility of falling in which the brothers teased me about all the time. In addition to all this, I had never spent one night away from my parents in the nearly five years of my life. This was nothing less than a major emotional trauma for me.

Maude may have intended to spend two weeks visiting her family, but that is not what happened. She and her boyfriend (my father's childhood friend) had broken up, and she had no place to live. So she stayed with her parents much longer than planned.

Weeks passed by without me seeing or speaking with my parents. Maude had promised that as soon as we arrived, she would call my parents and give them the telephone number for her parents' new house. Unfortunately, she never called them from their home, and I don't even believe they had a telephone.

For six weeks, my parents had no idea where I was. My mother called the state police in Alabama to request their help in locating me, but you can imagine how inclined they were to look for a small Black child from Connecticut on a farm in some unknown part of their state. This was a traumatic experience for me, but it was far more traumatic for my parents because they weren't sure where I was or when I would be returned home.

It wasn't until late July that Maude thought to call my parents from a church to inquire if it was "okay" for her to take me in "to view an Uncle who had died that day." Apparently the town didn't have a funeral parlor that would bury Black people so the deceased had to be buried immediately usually following a brief ceremony at a church. Fortunately, Maude had called collect, which gave my parents a telephone number. Agnes told Maude that if she did not have herself and me on a northbound train within 24 hours, she could expect the Alabama State Police arriving to arrest her for kidnapping. Agnes actually believed that the state police would do such a thing for me.

Maude realized that she was in trouble. We were bound for New York City within less than 24 hours because the money my parents wired for the train tickets came much sooner than that. As I explained before, my father had purchased round trip tickets the day we left New York City, but she turned in those tickets for a refund before we left for Alabama.

My father met our train when we arrived in New York City, and what he saw was extremely upsetting. It was obvious that I had lost a lot of weight, I appeared to be in poor health, and I showed signs of being traumatized. Maude failed to bathe me the entire time I was with her. My parents found a dark ring around my neck from not being washed, ears full of wax, and my hair wasn't combed the whole time I was away. My mother later told me that I did wash my face and hands and brush my teeth as she had taught me.

My mother also discovered lumps all around my waist. She immediately took me to my pediatrician who explained that the lumps were ticks that had climbed up my legs. The waistband on my panties stopped them from moving beyond my waist, so they buried themselves into my skin. He had to use a scalpel to dig them out one by one. It's amazing to me that I never developed lime disease.

Needless to say, I was quite a different child when I returned home. I was outgoing, friendly, happy, and even-tempered before they sent me on that long journey. I returned withdrawn, sullen, non-verbal, and I would wake up crying from reoccurring nightmares. Before I went away I was an only-child who was pampered by my parents and "aunties." They fussed over me and dressed me in adorable pink clothes per my preference. I felt "cute as a button," which is what I often heard everyone saying. When my mother found the dark circle around my neck, her uproar about me not bathing made me feel embarrassed. I was also upset because my mother had to cut my hair very short because the tangles and matting were too difficult to comb through.

Even worse was the pain associated with digging out the ticks that had buried themselves into my waistline.

The trauma of being separated from my parents was horrendous, but to return home and find my baby sister comfortably snuggled and settled into my home had to be emotionally challenging. My parents told me that I never seemed to resent my younger sister, and that I always behaved very sweetly towards her. Still, I wonder what I truly felt deep down inside. She was born on June 19th—the day before my birthday. That year there was no notice of my birthday by anyone in Alabama, which was quite different from my usual experience. I'm sure I was aware that my birthday had come and gone without fanfare.

My parents tried everything to bring back the little girl they had sent to Alabama. Up until that year, my birthday was a major celebration with my "aunties" and "uncles" standing in for the family that wouldn't participate. After that year, we celebrated my birthday as though it was a state occasion. My parents hosted huge backyard barbecues for my sister and me. My mom made sure we each had our own birthday cakes and individual big gift surprises.

Other occasions were elaborate as well. It was primarily because I was no longer an only child and the trauma I had experienced while I was away was very evident by my affect. My parents also knew that I still had to learn about being adopted so they, along with my aunties and uncles, exerted every effort to make me feel wanted and loved. They bent over backwards to prove to me that they never wanted to lose me or preferred their second child over me. But none of these gestures made a difference in my emotional status.

My depressed affect, anxiety and nightmares continued for years. In the middle of my eighth year, my parents decided to send me to the child psychologist, Dr. Kleeman, whom I mentioned at the beginning of this story. They wanted the doctor to explain to me that I was adopted (before the church community busy-bodies did) because they were too anxious about bringing up the topic after my visit to Alabama. Mostly, they were worried about my inability to interact comfortably with strangers, my feelings of insecurity and loss of self-esteem, and my loss of joy in life.

When I shared this part of my story over the years, many women worried that I experienced another kind of trauma while in Alabama. However, although Maude's brothers weren't within my age range as "playmates," they weren't dishonorable. They never placed a hand on me in any inappropriate manner. For that, I am grateful.

Another traumatic effect from that experience still occurs when I have to drive to an unknown place or by an unfamiliar route. I experience extreme anxiety as though I might fall off the face of the earth. Many years later in psychotherapy, my therapist and I traced that fear directly to that train ride in 1948. To this day, I have to talk myself through the process of getting someplace new. I make lots of plans, learn landmarks, get maps, etcetera to quiet the anxiety. I tell myself that I still haven't fallen off the planet. I also remember that Maude may have left me alone in the dark on that train, but I got to Alabama and I also got back to Connecticut.

WHAT WERE THE FACTORS THAT MAY HAVE LEAD MY PARENTS TO MAKE THIS DECISION?

How that traumatic experience could've happened is still a mystery to me. I believe that when my parents heard Maude mention a "new farm house," and "lots of land," and "younger brothers," they might have thought of a cute little New England farm house with a white picket fence surrounding it, a large backyard with a swing and fruit trees, and little boys who would be my playmates. Still, even to this day, this plan seems completely unreal to me. How could two parents who took me with them everywhere they went—social activities and vacations, NAACP meetings, church every Sunday, on regular outings to the market, pharmacy, doctor appointments, and the barber shop—decide to send their five-year-old to Alabama with someone who was a stranger?

There were older women at my parents' church who knew my father, his brother, their parents, as well as their grandparents. My parents could've asked one of them to take care of me during the day while my father was at his shop, and then he could've handled my care overnight. Then again, at the time my mother was pregnant with my sister, they hadn't completely made it clear to me that I had been adopted. Their closest friends advised them to stop telling me I was adopted, and to start preparing me for having a sibling because I would no longer be the only child in the family with the world in the palm of my hand. My parents probably feared that one of those older women of the church would've spoken to me about my adoption or asked me questions that might have shocked or upset me. Everyone in my parent's social circle knew that my parents had adopted me, but no one knew any of the details associated with my adoption. My parents always believed that, based on the nature of the busybody, those churchwomen were itching to know where I came from. So I can understand that maybe relying on them to provide care for me during that time was out of the question.

Many years later, I asked my parents several questions about this experience. I wanted to know why they decided to send me away with a perfect stranger for what was supposed to be two weeks but stretched into six; why they hadn't at least brought Maude to New Haven to spend some time with me so I would become more familiar with her; why they didn't have exact contact information for where we would be staying; and why they thought we could travel in compartment cars when many of my father's friends were Pullman Porters, and he knew that Black people were not allowed to sit in compartment cars on trains heading south.

My parents became very emotional and quiet when I questioned them. They cried and shook their heads in what looked like despair. Their regret was tangible, and they were emotionally unable to completely answer my questions.

When I think about their plan, how they reacted when I asked them those questions, and the trauma I had experienced, I believe my mother tried to explain what happened in ways that would minimize some of the mistakes they had made. For example, it is possible that my father didn't buy compartment tickets, but my mother wanted me to feel as though they tried to make the trip as comfortable for me as they could.

During my adolescence, I thought I might gain some insight about my trip to Alabama from my godparents—Aunt Elsie and Uncle Pete, and Aunty Thelma and Uncle Rudy. From the time I was born, my parents consulted them about everything related to raising my sister and me. My parents trusted their opinions because they had been parents for many years before I was born. So I met with each of them and asked what they knew about my parents' plan.

I knew my godparents very well so I could gage from their reaction to my questions that they had some thoughts about what happened, but they were not going to share them with me. Instead, they suggested that I ask my parents and that was all they would say. I can only speculate about what they knew or what they thought about the plan, but I don't believe they thought it was a good idea, especially my Aunt Elsie who was a social worker. They were very intelligent people so it is hard for me to believe that they approved of the plan. It is also possible that they learned something from my parents that made it seem like the best plan given the circumstances.

Years later after I connected with Shirley, I still wanted to understand why my parents sent me to Alabama so I asked her what she knew about the trip. She, too, became very vague. She said, "I seem to remember that there was a time you were away, but I really don't remember where you went or why." From the way she said it, I knew I wouldn't get any further information from her.

I've discussed this "mystery" with many people throughout my adulthood. They have offered their ideas about why my very responsible parents would choose to do something so risky with me. Some suggested that maybe my biological father learned about me and demanded some compensation or even custody of me. So to end his demands, they hid me away at Maude's home or sent me to him via Maude with the hope that he would realize he was unable to provide care for me.

Some people believe that someone in my parents' social circle learned that my biological father was trying to gain custody of me and took matters into their own hands, making him "disappear" for good. My father was non-violent, but the people offering this idea thought that no one knew what close friends might do to protect me. All I know is, my biological father was never seen around New Haven again after my fifth birthday.

Others suggested my parents had changed their minds about adopting me since they were expecting their biological child. So when Maude offered to take me south with her, they thought she might like to keep me. I can confidently say out of all the suggestions people have offered, this was not the case.

Still the mystery took a strange turn in later years. In 1976, I found a letter Maude wrote to my parents while I was in Alabama. It had her last name on the envelope with her parent's home address as a P.O. Box number, and the name of the town. In the letter she stated, "June was making a good adjustment." The letter was dated about ten days into the six-week ordeal. What would I be "adjusting" to if I were to be there for a two-week visit? The weather? The lack of electricity and indoor plumbing?

My parents had told me they didn't know where Maude had taken me or even her last name, so I confronted my parents with this letter. My mother immediately started to cry while my father stood by helplessly. Again, I didn't get any answers. So this has remained a mystery to me for many years, and the people who might have known the details have since made their transition, including Shirley.

Recently, my daughter Robin helped me to look at this mystery from a different perspective. She reminded me that I've always been a very gregarious individual—very upbeat, happy-go-lucky, and open to interacting with all types of people. She shared that perhaps my parents felt overwhelmed with the lack of extended family support, the pregnancy, and the length of time my mother would be hospitalized. Maude seemed like a nice young woman and I enjoyed her company the day we met. She was connected to a gentleman my father had known since they were small children. She seemed to like me and spoke about a lifestyle I would enjoy even though they had no idea she wasn't being completely honest with them. And my parents may have thought of this journey in the same vein as providing me with an opportunity to go to summer camp where I would enjoy outdoor fun, other children, and a countryside environment. Robin posited that it is also possible that when they received the letter from Maude, Agnes wrote her back and demanded a telephone number and a return date. As for my "adjustment," she thought Maude could've been referring to how I was coping with being away from my parents and interacting with her family.

The major problem was—I wasn't adjusting. Her family paid no attention to me and made it clear that they wished I wasn't there. I was scared half to death all the time, miserable, and underfed. No one bathed me or combed my hair, and ticks were eating me. The best thing that happened while I was there was that Maude thought to get permission from my parents to take me to a funeral. I often wonder what would've happened if she hadn't done that. How much longer would I have been in Alabama?

I'd like to take the more positive perspective, but I can't help the nagging thoughts that are still in the back of my mind. My parents should've researched more about Maude or checked with her boyfriend since he was an old friend of my fathers. They might have learned that they had stopped living together and the relationship had ended. He might even have been able to share more information about Maude and her background. They should've also insisted on having reliable contact with Maude or her parents in Alabama before allowing me to leave with her. I do believe they had good intentions, but many things out of their control went wrong.

A humorous (although somewhat sad) aspect about this situation was that during the six weeks I was in Alabama, lots of family and friends would come to spend a few days with Maude's family in their new farmhouse. When it was time for them to leave, Maude's mother would always pack up some of her homemade fried chicken and chocolate cake for them to take on the train. I looked forward to the day I would get some of this fried chicken and chocolate cake because I wasn't served any while I was there.

Once we boarded the train on our return journey, I asked Maude if I could have some chicken and cake. She told me her mother "had made us bologna sandwiches but no cake." There hasn't been a time in my life when I have eaten fried chicken and chocolate cake that I haven't remembered Maude and those train rides as well as the neglect and rejection I experienced in Alabama.

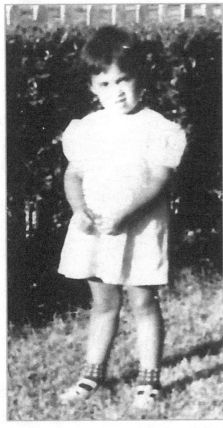

June at five years (1948) shortly after returning from Alabama

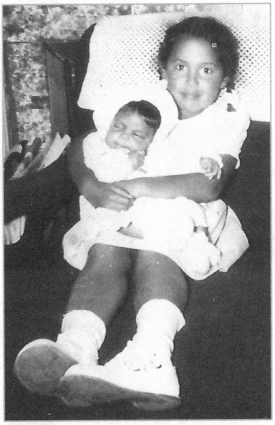

June at five years holding her baby sister Cathy, Fall of 1948

June's first piano recital, age 7, Milford, CT, 1950

June at the Girl Friend's Debutant Ball with escort Stanley Carnegie, New Haven, CT, December, 1960

June at the Milford High School Senior Prom with her date "Tiny" Johnson, who was a student at Yale University, May, 1961

June at age 29 at a Long Island, NY garden party

CHAPTER NINE
The Rest of My Childhood

The psychologist I saw for six months when I was eight years old not only helped me understand that I was adopted, but I gained a more positive sense of myself.

I became a Brownie during that school year, which also helped to restore my sense of belonging. The Scout Master for my troop was loving, affectionate, insightful, and inclusive. I'm sure she recognized that I had some emotional challenges, although she was not privy to what the situation was. Nevertheless, she was very gentle and kind. I was already acquainted with her because her oldest daughter and I were the same age, and we had been in school together for two years. I was very fond of her and her mother.

When I was nine years old, I joined the Girl Scouts. My new Troop Master was the exact opposite of my Brownie Scout Master, but she fueled my activism. I was always exposed to political activism through my parents' membership with the NAACP and my mother's fierce determination to never allow anyone to discriminate against her family. Being a Girl Scout gave me the confidence to stand up for my own rights.

During 1952, The NAACP staged a boycott against the Ann Page Grocery Stores (locally known as the A&P). The boycott developed because they didn't hire any Black people. Additionally, the NAACP charged the chain with discriminatory treatment of Black customers while they were in the stores. I joined the boycott wearing my Girl Scout uniform. We marched up and down in front of the A&P in Milford, Connecticut. I was photographed during the boycott, and the photo appeared in the Milford Citizen newspaper. My Scout

Master was furious. She called my mother and informed her that I was expelled from my Troop and from the Girl Scouts as a whole because I had "dishonored the Girl Scouts by participating in the boycott while wearing our uniform."

Let me just say that this woman did not know who she was dealing with. Agnes immediately called the State of Connecticut's Girl Scouts office and told them what the local Scout Master said about expelling me. They agreed with Agnes that the Troop Master's actions were improper. They said I had honored the Girl Scouts and my uniform by joining with those who were fighting for justice and against discrimination. The Troop Master was asked to resign, and my former Brownie Scout Master took over the Girl Scout Troop —much to my delight.

Participating in the boycott as a member of the NAACP against a store from which even I had experienced discrimination while shopping; having supportive parents; garnering the support of my State's Executive Director of the Girl Scouts; and having my photo in the newspaper as someone to be proud of and not ashamed of helped me heal from the experiences I suffered at age five.

That healing process from the trauma went on for many years and is probably still occurring. I am proud to say that I frequently engaged in psychotherapy to address any lingering issues. Those issues are probably why I chose to become a professional psychotherapist and social work educator.

GROWING UP IN MILFORD AND INTO MY ETHNICITY

We moved to Milford, Connecticut when I was six years old, which is nine miles south of New Haven. Milford had a small African American population even though they along with the Native Americans who had settled in that part of Connecticut in the mid-1600s were the first true residents of the area. I was always the only African American in elementary through high school classes. At the beginning of each school year, I had to field the usual questions and snide comments about my "suntan." My classmates would make invasive gestures such as touching my arm or face, and reaching out to touch my hair while inquiring why it was "so silky."

I still managed to have a few friendships with my classmates during first through sixth grade. Things changed quickly when I grew older. While the White classmates enjoyed my company and I theirs, their parents made sure that I was not invited to their parties after we turned twelve and their social events became co-ed. Their parents would even tell me they didn't think I would have a good time at their daughter's or son's party "because I wouldn't have anyone to dance with." The obvious implication was I would not be dancing with their sons.

My mother anticipated this reaction from the parents of my White classmates. She saved me from having a broken heart after being excluded by the kids I had chummed around with for six years. She and my father spent hours traveling the nine miles between Milford and New Haven so that I could have a normal social life and meet other kids with whom I had things in common. Most of my friends in New Haven were other children at our church or the grandchildren of my father's older friends.

My parents took me on many trips into New Haven for educational events at the African American Institute or special events and dances. Of course, we attended church there nearly every Sunday. They also took my sister and me to New York City to visit the museums, ethnic neighborhoods and restaurants, and their friends who lived in every borough of the city. I became very familiar with New York and always planned to raise the children I hoped to have right there in the most culturally and ethnically diverse city in the USA.

High school also had its challenges. In 1961, I was one of eight Black students in the Milford High School graduating class of 384 students. The eight of us were good friends for most of our lives. My close relationships were with the kids in my neighborhood, Bobby, Billy and Lynwood Richards, Craig Mitchell, Jimmy and Janice Williams, and the Santos family. They had the same experiences I did when they turned twelve. However, they had connections and friends in Bridgeport, a city nine miles south of Milford, so they went there for social events with other African Americans.

We experienced many challenges at Milford High School due to racism. The teachers often treated us as though we were somewhat unusual. No two Black students were ever in the same class together during the four years we attended the school. All of us were excellent students—some were also athletes, accomplished pianists, singers, and dancers. Yet our career counselor told each one of us that we needed to enroll in the "General" track, which would lead us into trade careers. The counselor told me, "You are not college material and you will never be able to go to college, so you need to learn to type and take shorthand."

I don't know what happened in the homes of my classmates when they shared the information from the counselor with their parents. I only know that Agnes could hardly sleep that night and was at the school the next day with me in tow before it opened. I thought she was going to choke the school counselor for suggesting I shouldn't enroll in the College Prep track or that I wouldn't be going to college. But she bypassed the counselor and dealt directly with the principal. By the end of that day, the counselor enrolled me and the other seven Black students in the College Prep courses. That was the end of that matter as far as Agnes was concerned. However, I still sustained self-esteem damage from the teachers and counselors who always implied that I wasn't the right material for college prep courses. Their negative comments lingered in the back of my mind for a very long time.

There were many positive experiences in my young life that strengthened my sense of pride as an African American. My father played the piano and he loved the music that grew out of Black communities. My father, godfather, and family friends would sit around the record player and listen to some of the great blues singers and jazz musicians. They would discuss the type of chords used, the style of the performers, and the quality of the voices and phrasings. I would be at my Daddy's knee soaking it up. Sometimes, when I was very young, my father would let me stand on his feet so that I could dance with him. We had special times sharing our love of music each night when we washed and dried the dishes together. My father taught me how to harmonize as we sang some of the blues tunes that he taught me. Little did I know that these lessons in music appreciation and basics in harmony would one day come in handy.

During the eighth grade, two of my girlfriends and I decided to form a singing group. We began singing along with some of my doo-wop records. We learned that there was an annual amateur contest at the beginning of the school year in our high school, and we decided to enter it. Over the summer between eighth grade and our first year in high school, my friends came to my home most afternoons so we could practice. My father coached us on our harmonies, helped us to decide who would sing lead on different songs, and encouraged us to believe we could win.

When school began that fall, the first thing we did was go to the Music department and tell the Chairperson that we wanted to enter the amateur contest. We were a multi-ethnic and multi-cultural girls singing group and we called ourselves The Sharpettes. During the contest we sang a song called

"Suga Wooga". I sang lead and my two friends backed me up. We won that contest! From that day on, we were invited to sing with the school band, The Sharptones, at many shows at the school and local sock hops around the community. My father, along with the band leader, nurtured my love for doo-wop music and singing. Winning that contest became one of my prize memories. It also contributed to my growing self-confidence and self-esteem.

Mrs. Edna Baker Carnegie, who established the African American History Institute, also fostered my self-pride. Edna was the sister of Justice Constance Baker Motley, the first African American female Federal District Judge appointed by President Lyndon B. Johnson. These two sisters were members of my family's church, St. Luke's Episcopal Church. When my father and his brother, Douglas, were pre-teens, they used to babysit young Edna and Connie after Sunday school during the 11 a.m. service. I grew up knowing these two dynamic women very well. To me, they were Aunt Edna and Aunt Connie. In fact, Edna's son Stanley escorted me to the Girlfriend's Debutante Ball in the fall of 1960.

Edna was one of the first African American public school teachers in New Haven, and she had a passion for Black history. She was able to gain support from Yale University to establish the African American History Institute. At least one Saturday per month—from the time I was ten years old until I graduated from high school—my parents took me to the Institute for lectures and lessons on Black history. Edna recommended books that featured the accomplishments that Black Americans, Africans, and people from the Caribbean had made throughout history.

My godmothers, Elsie Harris and Thelma Francis, introduced me to books I would never have read—books by and about W.E.B. DuBois, Zora Neal Hurston, Jean Toomer, Nella Larson and so many others of the Harlem Renaissance. It isn't that my parents hadn't exposed me to these brilliant scholars, but kids tend to listen more to others than to their own parents. And my parents and their friends believed in and practiced the old adage that "it takes a whole village to raise a child."

My father's aunt, Daisy, used to take me to the Yale University's Repertory Theater to see plays. She enjoyed teaching me how to dress for the theater, and she took me shopping for special outfits to wear to the theatrical productions. These excursions fit in well with my mother's plan for me to become a perfect example or representation of a lovely little Black girl. As I had stated, my parents took me all over New York City to learn about the varied cultures and ethnicities there. We sampled food from all around the world. We went to the ballet, theater, and symphony. Most importantly, we visited Wells Chicken and Waffles in Harlem for Sunday morning brunch after church. Yes, I eventually got my fried chicken!

My godfather Pete Harris was a graduate of Yale University, earning a master's degree in biochemistry. He worked as a researcher at Yale, helping to develop a better understanding of sickle-cell anemia and treatments for the condition. He is the reason Justice Thurgood Marshall became a part of our social circle. Marshall was frequently at Yale lecturing, researching, and networking. His primary Research Associate was Attorney Constance Baker Motley, our very own "Aunt Connie." As an attorney, she was instrumental in helping to prepare the school desegregation case *Brown vs. Topeka* that Attorney Marshall won before the Supreme Court. She went on to establish a distinguished career as one of the lead attorneys for the NAACP's Legal Defense and Educational Fund, winning many cases that desegregated schools and colleges across the South.

Another wonderful source of Black history and literature was Langston Hughes. He used to come to New Haven with friends he made in New York City who were from New Haven. He visited the Institute Aunt Edna established and St. Luke's Church. He also visited my family and many others in my parents' social circle for holidays or for brunch after church. I remember him as being hilarious, but at the same time very serious. He especially loved the Institute Edna had created and her dedication to promoting an understanding of where we came from and who we are. Mr. Hughes was delighted with Uncle Pete's devotion to the children around New Haven. Uncle Pete was godfather to many, and he spent a lot of time educating us and taking us to historic sites around New Haven and New York City.

These incredible individuals exposed me to people, places, events, and literature that many of my peers in college didn't know about. During the 1960s, it was amazing to me that my Black friends who graduated from college were talking about needing to develop a positive self-image. They shouted "Black Power" slogans and bragged about books they were just discovering—books I had already read. I realize now that being a young child around older adults meant that I benefited from their willingness to introduce me to things they hadn't been able to share with their children. It is very much like how grandparents have the time and patience to do things with their grandchildren that they didn't do with their children.

Most of the children in my social circle had this same type of hands-on education from people like Uncle Pete, Aunt Edna, Aunt Connie, and their famous and extremely accomplished friends, in the same vein as what W.E.B. Du Bois wrote about in Souls of Black Folks. As a matter of fact, Dr. Du Bois' grandfather Alexander Du Bois was one of the Founders of our church, St. Luke's Episcopal Church in 1845. My parents made sure that my sister and I knew whom we were and whose we were. As a teenager, each time I left home to go to a social event in New Haven, my parents would say, "Remember who and whose you are." They helped us understand that our behavior reflected on our family. They instilled a strong sense of pride in my sister and me, and for that I'm tremendously grateful. However, there were many challenging times before I was grounded with a fully developed sense of myself as a Murray from New Haven—a child of proud ethnically diverse parents who raised me well. Thankfully, those challenges brought enlightenment and commitment.

I moved away from Connecticut following my graduation from high school and so did most of my friends in New Haven. The few I'm still in contact with have experienced happy and successful lives. We thank our parents for preparing us educationally, politically, and spiritually for the battles we had to fight in the 1960s and 1970s.

I began college at Boston University in the fall following my high school graduation. My initial career in college was short lived for many reasons. The primary reason is that I freaked out myself by earning good grades. I earned A's in my Business Law, Accounting, and Economics classes, and B's in my Political Science and Spanish classes. I had nightmares that the Dean of Students called me into her office to tell me there was an error—that someone else's grades were accidentally placed on my transcript, and that I had only earned Cs or Ds, or worse yet, had failed my courses.

Why was I so freaked out about getting good grades? The self-esteem issues I developed at Milford High School from the teachers and counselors implying I wasn't the right material for college prep courses were still with me. The sense that I might not belong in college was a huge problem, and it lingered with me a very long time.

I got engaged by the end of my first semester of college. I dropped out of school and began preparing for my wedding, which disappointed my parents more than I could've ever imagined. I was still involved in the Civil Rights Movement and actively engaged in protest sit-ins. I served as a volunteer for the Fair Housing Authority in Boston, and joined the Boston University students who were organizing protests.

I married later that year and we had our two children by 1964. My children stimulated a renewed focus on my adoption and heritage. This began when my son, our first child, was born. His skin color looked like mine, but his hair was a much lighter shade of brown and his hairline was blond. I began to ask my parents questions about my biological parents. I wanted to learn more about my biological background, the history of my birthparents, and what to expect with regards to health. With each session of questions, my mother would contact Shirley and gather the information I asked about. They had shared with me that my birthmother was Irish and I assumed she had dark hair and dark-brown eyes. But I learned she actually had light-brown hair (like my son's) and intensely blue eyes. Also, many people in her family were strawberry-blond or blond with blue or green eyes. Shirley didn't have any information about my birthfather's family.

My children's genesis of personalities also became interesting to me as they were growing and expressing themselves. Sometimes I thought I would see aspects of their father's personality or mine in them, but many times their personalities didn't seem to match ours at all. This piqued my interest in the genes I was passing on to them.

This led me to learn more about recessive genes. I learned that you could never assume that two parents—one light and one of a darker hue—would produce a child somewhere in the middle with regard to complexion. Both of my children were as light as I was at my birth even though my biological father and my husband had darker complexions. As a child, my daughter's hair would turn quite red in the summer, which goes back to her biological maternal grandmother's family genes. I learned that my hair looks exactly like my maternal grandmother's who, unlike other members of her family, had thick dark-brown hair.

Throughout my life, these features have garnered intrusive and insensitive questions about my ethnicity because my appearance didn't fit what many Caucasians typically thought of as African American (or "Colored," as we were called in the 1940s). For example, a common question people would ask was, "What are you?" This sort of question often came from many African Americans as well. My hair was too straight, my skin color too light, my dialect too "White," and my neighborhood too "upper class" to qualify me as an African American in the minds of many people.

My mother had a different issue. She was Italian so she didn't look like the Anglo-Saxons that dominated Connecticut. She had a darker complexion and her hair and eyes were dark brown. People weren't always sure about her ethnicity—a factor she loved. If given the opportunity, she would tell people her grandmother was Black, which was not true at all. She even got a permanent in the 1960s that made her hair very curly. She wanted to fit in, to be a part of the Black community, to be accepted.

My mother's tendency to reject her ethnic heritage and her wish to be accepted by her Black friends based on her appearance inhibited me from accepting myself as I physically appeared. Years of feeling apologetic and guilty for being "light, bright and damn near White" combined with my own longing to belong, led me to feel uncomfortable around some Black women. I was especially uncomfortable around those who had sold a lot of "wolf-tickets" because they believed I thought highly of myself based on my appearance. This experience frequently occurred during my adolescence. I attended many social events in New Haven with large groups. I knew most of the girls and boys at the events, but there were also girls from the community I didn't know. Some of them would corner me in the ladies room and make negative comments based on their assumption that I had a certain attitude that stemmed from the value they assumed I placed on my skin color and hair texture. It was often frightening and would leave me feeling guilty about my appearance—until one significant day in Harlem in 1972.

I divorced in 1967 and in 1968, I moved with my two children from Boston to New York City and was thoroughly enjoying life. In 1972, I was dating a jazz musician. While he was in Europe on tour, he called to let me know that his new album had just arrived in record stores. He asked me if I would pick up a copy for him. I was excited about this news and agreed to help. I jumped out onto Broadway and grabbed a bus headed north to 125th Street and 7th Avenue.

When I got off of the bus, I encountered two African American teenage girls who physically stopped me and asked what I was doing in "their" neighborhood. One of the girls said, "Didn't you know that White people weren't welcome here?" I felt threatened because they towered over me and out-weighed me by about 100 pounds each. I engaged their madness and tried to convince them that I wasn't White. They weren't having it. They continued to push me and repeated that I needed to get out of their neighborhood. Suddenly, I got the harebrained idea to show them a photo of my father to prove I was Black. Once they realized that I was telling them the truth or a half-truth at any rate, they went crazy. They became even more determined to get me out of their neighborhood. It was bad enough when they thought I was White, trespassing in their territory. Once they realized I was actually Black that made them angrier. I didn't understand their perspective and the depth of what I came to learn was their internalized self-hatred, which was based on the accepted standard of "beauty" that in their opinion they did not fit. I had a lot to learn.

They whipped out a straight-edge razor and proceeded to grab a lock of my hair while shouting at me, "Oh yeah? Well…we'll see how Black you are when we cut off your hair!" During this ruckus, I noticed a patrol car with two police officers parked across the street. The officers seemed to be watching these young women and from what I could tell, had seen everything. I beckoned to them to come to my rescue and they immediately turned on their red and blue lights and siren, and swung around to my side of the street. They got out of their patrol car, grabbed the young teens, and one officer said, "Yeah, we've had trouble with these two before. They have mental health issues…don't worry." They threw the girls into the patrol car and drove off.

By that time, a group of people had formed around me so I pulled a tool out of my survivor skills toolbox that I didn't even know I had. I looked like the boldest soul sister you have ever encountered, and stared into the faces of those in the crowd with a dare. I walked straight towards them then across the sidewalk and across 125th Street down Broadway and all the way home to 106th Street and West End Avenue purely on adrenalin.

I thank the Lord that this happened on a cold day in March rather than a sultry, humid day in August because I might not have survived the experience. This act saved my life—not to imply that my life was in danger by the crowd because the attention span of most New Yorkers with incidents not directly affecting them is very short—it saved my life in another way. From that day, I've never worried about anyone else's perspective about my hair texture, skin color, economic background, or educational status that is used to initially frame their opinion about me. As people get to know me, they realize I don't assess those things as aspects of my character or theirs.

My formal education, which included studies in African American history and culture, along with joining discussion groups and participating in televised interviews with authors who have studied skin color bias among African Americans, helped me to become more educated about the learned behavior that has conditioned African Americans to value one skin color over another. We have been conditioned to negatively compare ourselves with the dominant standard of "beauty," which goes back to the era of slavery and Jim Crow.

I am a part of the generation of cultural educators and mental health clinicians that have tried to help members of our communities unlearn the tendency to negatively evaluate the grade of our hair or the size of our bodies, lips, nose, etc. None of these aspects should be considered in evaluating who we are as human beings. We have internalized these negative opinions historically forced upon us by society, and I am committed to supporting the process of unlearning these messages. I share with others what my parents taught me—"hair does not have character so it can be neither good nor bad." My parents also taught me to believe in what Martin Luther King, Jr. believed —your character is what's important, not whether you are a particular shade of black, brown, or white!

RESETTING MY GOALS

Between 1961 and 1976, my parents, godparents, and close friends encouraged me to return to college. I believed I had several barriers preventing me from earning a college degree. First was the fear that I had been out of school too long and wouldn't do well, which stemmed from the insecurity my career counselor in high school had fostered. Next was the fact that I was a single parent raising two children in New York City. My parents and sister Cathy were always there to help and my children's father contributed to their support as well, but it still seemed like a huge hurdle. And while I was able to find employment, I never earned enough to afford college tuition. Most importantly, I felt that returning to school would require a lot of time and make me unavailable to my children, and I didn't want that for them.

It took fifteen years of struggling in the workforce to make up my mind. I had many jobs beginning with a bookkeeper position at Columbia University in the Office of Student Activities, which I held for about one week. It was a nightmare because I had zero skills to carry out my responsibilities as a bookkeeper. I met my friend, Jonathan King, during that scary time and he introduced me to Dr. Julian Miller, Columbia's Chair of the Graduate Chemistry Department. Those two gentlemen saw the dilemma I was in and guided me into a position that I could handle. Dr. Miller gave me time off to care for my children, Jonathan babysat my children, and they enabled me to survive during my first year in New York City. I continue to be grateful for Jonathan's friendship and that of his lovely wife Ellen.

The sexism and racism that I experienced in my last two jobs made me realize I could and should return to college. In 1976, I enrolled in the State University of New York – College at Old Westbury as a nontraditional, full time student. I tried to involve my children, who were then twelve and thirteen years old, as much as possible so they could share the experience with me.

That was the first of fourteen years of pursuing a multidisciplinary/multicultural education that resulted in earning three master's degrees—the first at Columbia University in the School of Social Work as a Family Therapist and concluding with a PhD in Ethnic Studies and Psychology at the University of California – Berkeley. While studying for my second master's through my PhD, both of my children were enrolled in college then graduated. My son Cole graduated from California State University at San Jose. He later graduated from Boston University's School of Social Work, specializing in Gerontology. My daughter Robin graduated from Mills College in Oakland, California then Duke Law School in Durham, NC. My parents were able to attend my college graduation as well as my children's graduations from high school and college. Their pride in our accomplishments was nearly tangible.

June as an undergraduate student with Dr. Eric Erickson at a Research Seminar, Middlebury, VT, 1978

June's graduation day from Columbia University School of Social Work with her daughter Robin, 1982

June with close friend and SUNY Old Westbury classmate Mercedes Rosas, Milford, CT, 1984

June with her two children, Cole and Robin, at her PhD graduation from U. C. Berkeley, Berkeley, CA, 1991

June hosting an old friend, Kwame Toure, (a.k.a. Stokely Carmichael) at North Carolina State University, Raleigh, NC, 1993

June meeting Iron Sculptor, Phillip Simmons, in Charleston, SC, 1994

June with her U.C. Berkeley Professor, Dr. Ron Takaki, pointing to their friend Dr. Michael Eric Dyson, together for a panel discussion/seminar on Multicultural Studies at Duke University, Durham, NC, 1995

June with Mentor, Dr. John Hope Franklin, hosted by Gov. and Mrs. Jim Hunt of the State of North Carolina, Raleigh, NC, 1996

June joking with
Mentor/friend,
Dr. Maya Angelou,
Winston Salem, NC,
2000

June with a colleague,
Dr. T. Alex Washington,
of the Social Work
Department - University
of Maryland – Morgan
State Campus,
Baltimore, MD;
photo taken in 2010

June's "adopted" niece
Philipina Kwashie. They
met in Ghana, West
Africa while June was a
visiting professor at the
University of Ghana –
Legon; photo was
taken in 2018

Andrew,1986

Agnes, 1987

Three generations – June with her mother Agnes and her daughter Robin;
Berkeley, CA, 1987

CHAPTER TEN
"Don't You Want to Meet Your "Real" Parents?

When I was thirteen, my mother and I began discussing some of the details of my adoption and she shared that I could meet with my birthmother whenever I wanted. Well, let me rephrase this, out of one side of her mouth she would say, "Your birthmother is right there in New Haven, and anytime you want to meet her just let me know and I can set it up." Out of the other side of her mouth I felt she was saying, "Oh no! Please don't want to see her, care about her, or love her."

So I always said, "Thanks, but no thanks!" I also thought why should I want to request a meeting with her? If anyone makes a request, it should be her. She's the one who gave me away!

Over the years, many people would ask me, "Don't you want to meet your real parents?" They would be referring to my biological parents and my stock answer would always be, "I have absolutely no interest in meeting them." And I believed this was true.

Then I had a hysterectomy when I was 43 years old. I did not have cancer, but the surgeon requested that I check with my biological mother about any cancer in the family to establish a base line for me. I was living in California so I called my mother in Milford and asked her to call Shirley and inquire about anyone in her family who may have experienced cancer, especially any women. My mother agreed to this request and promised to call back soon with any information she learned.

She called about two hours later and shared that she spoke with Shirley and learned that no one had cancer. My mother sounded odd so I asked if there was any other news or was she upset about something. She began to cry as she related more of her conversation with Shirley. It happened that Shirley's older sister had recently died and she was the last sibling in her family who might have guessed that the first baby Shirley had didn't die but may have been given away for some reason. Shirley told Agnes that she was "now free to openly connect with June." She asked Agnes to tell me that she "wanted to see me and to develop a relationship with me" and "hoped that I would call her." I asked my mother why she was crying and if she thought Shirley was going to wheel me away in my baby carriage. My mother simply but tearfully replied, "Yes." I told her the same thing I told everyone else—that I had no interest in connecting with or seeing Shirley and to stop worrying. But I think a tiny seed was planted in my mind.

During the next seven years between 1986 and 1993, my mother suffered multiple debilitating strokes. The last one left her completely immobile, as well as being unable to eat normally or to speak. In addition to my great concern for her was the subconscious understanding that she and Shirley would no longer have any contact with each other. My father had passed in 1991 so I didn't have to worry about how he might feel about me connecting with my birthmother.

Three months after my mother became disabled I had a dream. In my dream, I sensed that it was time for me to go to New Haven to find my birthmother. So I walked into a storefront where I believed she would be. There, I found three older White women with sparkly white hair. They were sitting in a row in straight-back chairs. The store was completely empty except for some shelves on one wall. The women said hello to me and asked if they could help me. I told them that I was looking for Shirley Cushion. Their facial expression changed to sadness. Then one of them asked if I was a friend of hers. I paused a moment then said, "Well…yes, I guess you could say that." This woman went on to say that Shirley wasn't there anymore and that she had died three months earlier. The woman wanted me to know that Shirley's last few years were the happiest and most economically comfortable years of her life. She shared that Shirley's daughter had married a psychologist by the name of Tom Zipper who welcomed Shirley into the home he shared with his wife, and that the couple had adopted a child which Shirley took care of for the first three years of his life. I thanked her for this information and backed out of the door. I walked past the store's front window, turned the corner of the building out of the sight of the women, then fell against the building and began to sob.

I woke up from the dream with the front of my nightgown sopping-wet from my tears. That is when I realized I had been lying to myself for years. I did want to meet and connect with my birthmother.

That day I knew I had to call Shirley, but I had to mentally prepare for what may happen when I called her. I had been very much a psychic or clairvoyant—often seeing future events in dreams or suddenly having accurate knowledge about various things without any understanding how this would happen. So, I thought, what if my dream was accurate and Shirley had died? And even though seven years earlier Shirley had told my mother she was ready to have a relationship with me, I didn't know if it was still true and feared rejection again.

That morning, I went to the North Carolina State University campus and taught my summer classes as usual while pushing my dream to the back of my mind. As I drove home in the afternoon, the dream was very much in the front of my mind. I do my deepest thinking when showering or washing dishes because the water seems to make things clear in my mind. So I washed the dishes in my kitchen while planning a script for the telephone conversation with Shirley I felt certain I would have.

My mother always said that Shirley was in New Haven and I believed she lived on Davenport Avenue. In July of 1993, one could still call the telephone company's information service, and this is what I did. I asked the operator for Shirley Cushion on Davenport Avenue in New Haven, Connecticut. The operator informed me that she didn't see Shirley Cushion or S. Cushion listed. I thanked her, hung up, and washed more dishes.

I had a strong feeling that Shirley was there so I called information again. The second operator couldn't find her name or number either, but he asked me how I spelled the last name. I hadn't seen Shirley's last name in print since I was 13 years old when my sister found that little newspaper article. I assumed the spelling was like a chair cushion. I told him, "C-U-S-H-I-O-N."

He paused a minute then said, "There's another spelling and I see a Shirley Cushen on Central Avenue."

I knew that Central Avenue was off of Davenport Avenue so I took the number from the operator and immediately dialed it. I was shocked when she answered and I heard the sound of her voice. She sounded just like Agnes who had a deep, husky, and distinctive voice. The similarity in their tones came from being long-term smokers. I almost hung up because the nonsensical thought that ran through my mind was what is Agnes doing at Shirley's house? Another problem was my script. After I said, "Hello, may I speak with Shirley," I had nothing! And Shirley sounding like Agnes threw me for a loop.

There was a long pause then she responded tentatively in my mother's voice, "This is Shirley."

I said, "Is this the Shirley who knows Agnes and Andrew Murray?"

There was another long pause. "I know Agnes and Andrew," she finally said.

"Shirley, this is June," I said.

There was a really long pause this time then she said, "June! Oh my God! I have wanted to talk to you for 50 years!" This time her voice completely changed and now sounded exactly like mine! She continued, "How are you? Are you okay? How is Agnes? I know your father died recently. Is Agnes okay? Oh June, I can't believe I'm finally hearing from you." She was excited, exuberant, and she sounded sincere. She even used words I would use. It was crazy. I was almost speechless and that's saying a lot.

We spent over two hours on the phone asking each other questions and catching up on our lives. Right before we ended the conversation, Shirley asked, "Why did you call me today?" I told her that I had had a dream. In a very serious, quiet, and almost mysterious tone of voice, she slowly replied, "Tell me about your dream." As I related every detail, she listened quietly then she said, "You have the gift. You have my mother's gift. You see the future don't you? You know things, right?" I agreed and she went on to say, "Your dream is fascinatingly accurate. Obviously I didn't die three months ago, but three months ago I did stop working in that storefront you saw in your dream. It is right down the street from our house. I had been selling yarn for my daughter who opened that store, so when she decided to close it that was an end for me in a way. Those women you saw are my friends. They live in the neighborhood and they would come and sit with me to keep me company. And they look exactly as you described them. My daughter did marry a psychologist and his name is Tom as in your dream. His last name is not Zipper—it's Kidder so you were close. And they adopted a son from Peru. His name is Danny and I did take care of him for the first three years of his life and still do. My son-in-law bought a three-family house. He and my daughter and grandson live on the first floor and I live on the second floor. They help me financially. Most of my life I have been very poor but since my daughter married Tom, he has helped me so much."

During that first conversation, I learned that Shirley and Sidney had four children. Two years after my birth they had a daughter, Beverly Raye, then two years later they had twin sons, Michael and Kenneth, and three years later they had another son, John. Of the twins, Kenneth died in Viet Nam. My mother had saved a photo from the New Haven Register newspaper from 1967 of Shirley marching in a parade protesting the Viet Nam War and honoring the fallen. My mother showed it to me when I was 24 years old. As I said, the story of my adoption and those who peopled my origin continued to unfold for many years.

Shirley also shared that her 22-year marriage to Sidney was wracked with anguish and trauma. Her husband never forgave her for being sexually involved with a Black man and would constantly bring it up. He demeaned her in front of their children without explaining what he was angry about, so they developed a general sense that he thought there was something wrong with their mother's character. She and Sidney divorced in 1968, which was the same year my divorce was finalized. Prior to her divorce, she was forced to move away from her children until she could gain custody of them. Shirley explained that leaving her home then divorcing her husband caused a major rupture in her relationship with John. She believed he never recovered from it. Over the next seventeen years, I saw that this caused Shirley a great deal of emotional pain.

Towards the end of our first conversation, Shirley said she was very happy I called her. We made plans to talk again soon, which we did. We often wrote each other, sharing our life experiences and answering each other's questions. I didn't tell anyone, except my two children, that I had gotten in touch with Shirley. I was afraid that someone would tell my mother and she would be very upset.

I visited Shirley the following November. We went to the storefront where her daughter had a yarn shop, and it looked exactly like it did in my dream. Beverly Raye, a Virgo, opened the yarn shop because she knits and crochets and was tired of spending so much money on yarn in retail stores. My daughter, whose birthday is one day after Beverly Raye's, also knits and crochets very beautifully. I also learned that Beverly Raye went to Columbia University School of Social Work. She was there to earn her PhD in Administrative Social Work while I was earning my Masters in Clinical Social Work. We were there at the same time, but we didn't know each other. We could've passed each other in the hallways and never suspected that we shared genetics. Coincidences? I hardly think so.

MEETING SHIRLEY'S FAMILY

Shirley shared with me that when my mother called her seven years earlier to inquire about any history of cancer in her family, she decided to tell Beverly Raye that she had a baby and had given me up for adoption to Agnes and Andrew. On the first day Shirley and I spoke, Beverly Raye came into her home while we were on the phone and Shirley told her that she was talking to me. Beverly Raye's reaction to this news didn't feel positive to me even though she knew it was the first time Shirley and I were talking. I didn't say anything about my feelings or suspicions, but I later found out it wasn't just a hunch. Shirley eventually confirmed that Beverly Raye wasn't sure about her feelings towards her mother connecting with me.

Shirley vacillated for several months about telling her two sons and their wives and children about me. I didn't care at first, but gradually it began to bother me. I felt I was still being treated like a negative secret. I decided to tell Shirley that if she couldn't be open about me at this point then our short-lived relationship was over. On that same day, before I could tell her about my feelings, she told me that her daughter had scolded her for keeping me a secret from her siblings. So she planned to meet with her sons and their families to tell them the whole story. Shirley laughed when I told her why I had called and suggested that we were on the same "wave length." What I didn't tell her was that I was surprised it was her daughter who stressed that she should stop keeping me a secret from her siblings. I still felt as though Beverly Raye might not be excited about having an older sister pop into her mother's life. On the other hand, I also thought that as a social worker she would want to do the right thing regardless of her personal feelings. I tried to imagine how I would feel if our roles were reversed and what I might do. I was willing to not judge her and to wait and see how things would develop over time.

The week after Shirley's conversation about me with the rest of her immediate family, I received a phone call from her oldest son Michael. He informed me that he "loved" the fact that he had me as his "sister." He shared that when his mother called for a family meeting, he feared that she was going to tell them about some major health problem she was having, but was relieved she was sharing something he had suspected for years. He shared that he knew his father was implying something his mother had done that he thought was immoral, but his father never specified what that behavior was.

His response to me was quite different from his sister's, but their personalities were also quite different. Michael was warm, affectionate, and communicated openly and directly. I didn't hear from John immediately, but later I learned he was rather shy and wasn't very talkative. He seemed nonplused about me being his "sister" when we met, but Shirley thought his reaction to her after he learned about me was more in line with his father's. She felt he still judged her negatively.

In subsequent conversations with Michael, he shared that his mother was probably expecting her children and other family members to react about her becoming pregnant by a Black man as her parents and siblings would have reacted in 1942. But among her children and grandchildren there were many relationships with People of Color. Her daughter had adopted a son from Peru; Michael's son was married to an African American woman and their daughter was "mixed" as he put it; one of his nephews is also married to an African American woman; and before he was married, Michael had been seriously involved with a Cuban woman in Florida and they have a daughter together. So in his mind, Shirley had nothing to worry about with regard to being judged by her family. Michael frequently said he "felt bad to learn that while we were growing up he had another sister who had lived just miles away from him that he didn't know"

As for Sidney—Shirley's former husband and the man who was my legal father once I was born and who agreed to allow my adoption to legally proceed but whom I had never met—he died exactly six weeks after I connected with Shirley. Is this yet another coincident comparable to my mother's father dying six weeks after my adoption became legal and final by the State of Connecticut?

On July 4, 1995, Michael hosted a family cookout in his backyard to honor and introduce me to more members of his family. My son was traveling out of the country, but I was able to take my daughter with me. We were amazed at how much she and my son looked like many of the Cushen family members. The most amazing thing was how much my gestures and mannerisms were like Shirley's, which was something Michael and John continuously commented on. They noted that Shirley and I were physically built exactly alike as well.

Shirley, surrounded by her three children along with Robin and me, chatted all day and got to know one another. Michael and John asked my opinion about issues in their lives as though I was their big sister. Beverly

Raye's non-verbal reaction suggested she might not have liked not being the oldest of Shirley's children anymore. Michael even said that they would usually ask Beverly Raye about issues in their lives. Beverly Raye didn't have to worry though. It was never my intention to become a part of their family or be their older "sister." My goal was to learn more about my birthmother and her family of origin as well as her immediate family—not to join them.

One of the funniest things that happened at the gathering related to my love of doo-wop music. Shirley had told me that her son Michael was a deejay in his spare time. I thought that's nice, and told her that my son had also been a deejay in his spare time.

At one point during the cookout while Michael, John, Robin and I were sitting on his deck, Michael asked me what type of music I liked. Now I had been from coast to coast in this country trying to find someone who loved the music from the late 1940s thru the early 1960s, which was initially referred to as Rhythm and Blues but later renamed "Doo-wop". I hoped to find someone who knew more about that genre of music than I do and could reminisce with me about the street corner harmony groups, especially those out of New York City. So here was Michael, my half-brother, asking me about my favorite type of music. I thought to myself this country White boy probably likes that loud heavy metal or some variety of what I would call "country mess". Yes, I know I was being biased and shortsighted.

I said, "Oh, I am into doo-wop music," thinking he probably wouldn't know what I was talking about.

But Michael got excited and said, "Really? That's my music!"

Later he told me I had a smirk on my face and Robin agreed. I didn't mean to look that way, but I was thinking this man couldn't possibly relate to my music. No way! So I said, "Hmmm." And I'm sure it sounded dismissive.

Michael didn't let it bother him. He very kindly asked, "So, what is your favorite song?"

I thought let me put an end to this right here and now. I thought of a song that was rather obscure to most people unless they were really into doo-wop. I said, "The Wind."

Michael asked, "The Wind? Oh, what version? Which group?"

His question amazed me. I thought *uh oh*, and began to get nervous because I didn't even know another version existed other than the one by The Jesters. So I said, "The Jesters."

Michael nudged John and said, "She likes 'The Wind.'"

Before I could count to three, Michael and John began singing the song in perfect harmony. They knew all the lyrics—lyrics I didn't completely know despite the many times I had listened to that song.

Robin laughed hysterically and told me that she wished that I could have seen the expression on my face. Over the next seventeen years, Michael and I had many conversations about doo-wop music. We talked about the big stars and the recording labels. He shared that he had been a part of a doo-wop singing group in New Haven during his teens, and he was so excited to learn about my singing "career." He saw it as "genetic" and shared what he knew about Shirley's career as a professional jazz singer. Michael provided me with many cassettes of the music recorded from his collection, which far surpassed my own collection to the point that it was funny. He also gave me copies of his radio show for which he played doo-wop music as a deejay. During these exchanges with Michael, I learned important lessons about genetics and the embarrassing things that may happen when one is judgmental. Years later, I wished that I could share with Michael that I had become a deejay of doo-wop music on a local radio station in Charleston, SC.

Throughout my childhood the debate about nature versus nurture was waged in our social circle—nurture always being the side of the debate my parents favored. Their friends didn't always agree, especially Uncle Pete who was a Biochemist. I agreed with my parents until the birth of my grandson, and listening and observing Shirley and her children that day created a major change in my mind. My deep belief in nurturance versus nature was forever turned upside-down.

Although I had known for many years that my birthmother was Irish, meeting her and her family (my blood relatives) was difficult for me. I was raised to think of myself as only Black—not mulatto, mixed, or bi-ethnic even though it's genetically accurate. There wasn't any room in my mind for adapting to thinking of myself or being thought of as Irish. Culturally, I can't see myself as "half White."

Robin seemed to have accepted that part of her genetics very easily. She and Shirley discussed Ireland and what Shirley had learned from her parents about their culture. Years after learning that Shirley was a member of the 5th Irish generation from great-great grandparents who had immigrated from Ireland, Robin and my grandson Christopher visited the part of Ireland where Shirley's family originated, but they couldn't find anyone who knew of the O'Maras—Shirley's father's family.

One more interesting and I supposed ironic fact I learned from Shirley was that I lost a member of my biological family on the Titanic in 1912. Shirley told me her mother's uncle, James Kelly, was lost on the Titanic. He was the brother of Shirley's maternal grandfather John Kelly. Her great-uncle had a daughter, Margaret Kelly, who lived with her Kelly grandparents. Margaret had purchased a ticket for her father and mailed it to him, with an invitation for him to come to America and join her and his brother and family. He accepted her invitation and boarded the Titanic in Ireland, but unfortunately, he did not survive the ship's accident. Following her father's death, Margaret moved in with Shirley's parents and spent the next ten years living with them while helping to raise their children, including Shirley. Shirley had saved the newspaper articles about the tragic loss of her great uncle.

It was amazing to learn about this because ever since I first learned of that tragedy, I had been fascinated by the story. I watched and purchased every movie and documentary about the tragedy. I never could understand why I was so interested in the event. After hearing the story from Shirley, the mystery of my fascination with the Titanic was solved. Somewhere in the deep recesses of my subconscious was the knowledge that I had ties to the tragedy. While I never identified as Irish or half-Irish, there certainly are ties that can't be denied. I do believe in Jung's theory of the Collective Unconscious and this may be an example of it.

For the next 17, almost 18 years, I remained in touch with Shirley. I lived far away from Connecticut, but I saw her as often as I could. I made sure my children, grandson, sister, and my cousin Mary Corrine also spent time with Shirley and her family. In addition to Shirley's three children, I met her son-in-law Tom and grandson Danny. I also met several of her nephews and nieces at some major family gatherings, like Shirley's 80th birthday party. This later group was polite to me, but Shirley shared that behind the scenes they were telling her to be careful about connecting with me because I might want something from her. Shirley found it ironic because she knew that my children and I, based on our education and careers, couldn't possibly want or expect anything of monetary value from her. She also knew my parents and how I was raised, and my character and that of my two children wouldn't lend us to be dishonest. She expressed her chagrin that their concerns were based on racist stereotypes, and she apologized for their assumptions.

Shirley shared many times that she felt good about her decision to ask Agnes and Andrew to adopt me, and that it was obvious that they provided me with a life she couldn't have given me. She said if she had been able to keep me, my "life would have been miserable" due to her husband's bias against Blacks and her family of origin's similar sentiments. She made it clear that no one in her family would've welcomed me, and that they would've gone out of their way to reject me.

Many years after meeting Shirley, I moved to Las Vegas. Shirley arranged for me to meet her older sister's son—the one she called her "favorite nephew." At this point, he was in his 70's. He remembered being around his mother and listening to her discuss Shirley, especially during the summer of 1942 when he was twelve years old. He told me that a young man that Shirley was engaged to was killed in World War II. Following his death, she went through a period during which she grieved his loss. She was still very young and began to date again, but her sister thought her "behavior was disgraceful" so soon after her fiancé's death. Her nephew also remembered his mother and grandfather's reaction when Shirley married a Jewish man.

Her nephew shared that he heard his mother and Shirley talking about her pregnancy. Then they talked about the death of the child whom he was told was stillborn. However, he knew that his mother didn't believe the story. He once asked his mother why he didn't hear about the funeral for Shirley's baby. His mother told him to "mind his own business" and the topic was never discussed again. He said he suspected something else had happened, but it wasn't until after I had contacted Shirley in 1993 that she told him about me and my adoption.

He echoed Shirley's thoughts about the family's attitude towards African Americans. He made it clear that his parents, maternal grandparents, aunts, and uncles would have put Shirley out into the street if she had shared that she was pregnant by a Black man or if she wanted to keep his child.

I often think about the many things that are unexplainable coincidences between Shirley's life and my life. For example, Agnes' father kicked her out of his family when she married a Black man. When her mother learned that she and Andrew adopted me, her father refused to allow her mother to visit me. Then when I was six weeks old, Agnes' father died. Years later Shirley's husband died exactly six weeks after she and I connected. Another example is that Shirley's name is the same as Agnes' friend who made arrangements for Agnes to move to New Haven. That friend, Shirley, had a daughter by the name of Beverly, and my birthmother's daughter's name is also Beverly. Yet another coincidence is that my birthmother's mother's maiden name is Kelly, and my godmother—the one who rushed to the hospital to welcome me on the day I was born—was Elsie Kelly Harris. Another uncanny example is that my birthmother's favorite niece's name is Catherine, my paternal grandmother and my sister's name is Catherine, and I blessed my daughter with the middle name of Catherine. I also learned that Shirley's mother's first name was Elizabeth, and my father's paternal grandmother's name was Elizabeth too. Maybe the names being the same only reflect popular names at certain times in history, but maybe not.

June's first meeting with birthmother Shirley O'Mara Cushen, New Haven, CT, 1993

June with Shirley, New Haven, CT, 1995

Shirley with June and June's grandson Christopher, New Haven, CT, 2004

Margaret Kelly, New Haven girl whose father perished on Titanic.

PROMINENT CANADIANS ABOARD ILL-FATED SHIP

London, April 16.— A number of prominent Canadians were on board the Titanic at the time of the disaster. Among them were Mark Fortune, a capitalist of Winnipeg, who had been spending the winter on the Riviera; Hugo Ross, son of the late A. W. Ross of Winnipeg, a politician; and T. O. C. Caffry, the western superintendent of the Union Bank of Vancouver. All these are known definitely to have sailed.

PASSENGERS BOOKED WHO DID NOT SAIL

Southhampton, Eng. April 16 — The following passengers whose names were on the list of the Titanic did not embark:

First class — A. M. J. White, Mrs. Paul Schabert.

Second class — Dr. J. C. Jenkins, Mrs G. Wilkinson, Ada Wilkinson

The Mrs. Paul Schabert mentioned in the above despatch is a Derby resident and was previously reported as a saved passenger and aboard the Carpathis.

BOAT NEVER AT FULL SPEED
ISMAY SAYS, IN TRAGIC RECITAL

A speedy and merciless grilling of J. Bruce Ismay, general manager of the White Star line, who was a... ry," said Mr. Ismay. "This awful catastrophe I must say at the outset, I greatly deplore. We have nothing...

Newspaper article about June's relative – John Kelly – who was lost on the Titanic, 1912; Mr. Kelly was Shirley's great-uncle

Shirley lunching with June, New Haven, CT, 1995

Shirley and her brother Bill at a family picnic, New Haven, CT, 1995

June's sister Cathy with Shirley, New Haven, CT, 1996

June's son Cole with Shirley, New Haven, CT, 2009

June's father, Andrew; photo taken in 1939

CHAPTER ELEVEN
What About Your Father?

When people ask me this question, they are referring to my biological father. Agnes described him as being six feet, five inches, a deep reddish-chocolate brown color, hair "that laid down straight," slender through his hips, muscular, and very good looking. He told people that he was from New York City, but Agnes thought either he or his parents were originally from the Caribbean. She thought he might have been from Barbados or Nevis because he had an accent like many of the people from those countries that lived in New Haven. I don't know if there were other reasons why she believed he was from the Caribbean but based on my research, he did have a common Bajan name. What's interesting is whenever I visit Barbados, people there tell me I am "Bajan" and that I've "come home."

Agnes told me his name when I was 18, then Shirley confirmed his name when I was 50 years old. I admit there was a time when I thought it might be interesting to look him up to see who he really was. Between the age of 25 when I first moved to New York City and 60, I checked phone books in every city that I lived in or visited. I also inquired about his name when I visited Barbados. Recently my daughter looked up his name on a website for tracing one's genealogy, and all the entries were of White men. That made me wonder if he was an undocumented immigrant. Now that I live in Charleston, SC, I have learned that the local Gullah accent sounds very much like the accent one hears in Barbados and Nevis. So maybe he was from the Gullah/Geechee Corridor.

I had my DNA analyzed and found out that a large portion of my heritage stemmed from Nigeria. I also learned that people stolen from Nigeria were often taken to Barbados. Then many of those held in bondage in Barbados were brought to Charleston in the 1670s. So when people in Barbados see a trace of Bajan-esque in my face, they may be right. But it is also possible, based on my daughter's research, that the name I was given by Agnes and Shirley was incorrect. Then again, everyone in America is not listed in a genealogy search engine.

I have ambivalent feelings about finding my biological father or his descendants. Based on what Shirley told me, he didn't want anything to do with me (the embryo) or Shirley for that matter. Still my parents were relieved that Shirley had married before I was born so my biological father wouldn't have any legal claim on me. My parents believed he knew that my father was financially comfortable and had extensive resources. They weren't sure about his character but were advised by their friends who had briefly interacted with him to not take any chances. So my parents were concerned about possible demands he might have made if he learned that they had "his child."

When I was about two months old, my mother was walking down the street with me in my baby carriage. She saw my biological father about a block ahead of her. She spun the carriage around and went in the opposite direction. My mother knew he was aware she and Shirley were friendly. And although he no longer worked at the factory, she feared he would somehow realize that this baby she had in the carriage might be his child. My parents never saw him again after that incident, so they assumed he left New Haven.

Many years later while I was at my parents' 50th Anniversary party, I had a conversation with one of my father's best friends. I had heard he was one of the friends my father checked with about my biological father's character. My father's friend played the piano in some of the nightclubs that my biological father frequented, so he had observed him over a period of about a year. I asked this friend what he remembered about my biological father and his response was clear, swift, and direct. He said, "Nothing good. And you have the best father anyone could imagine having in Andrew Murray…keep that in mind!"

I never asked anyone else about my biological father until I connected with Shirley. Opening that door now would be like opening Pandora's box. I suspect that he would probably not agree that I was related to him, unless he thought there was some benefit for him to do so. Of course, this way of thinking could just be based on stories I've heard of other similar situations and not on fact. Still, I have no illusions about him having any regrets about that day Shirley told him she was pregnant, and he suggested she take some powder that might bring on her period. (I first learned of this exchange from Agnes then Shirley told me the same thing many years later.)

I would guess that he had other children and based on my experience from many years of providing family therapy, I'm not sure his children or grandchildren would welcome me with open arms. When I have discussed this scenario with friends, they agreed that it would be unusual that if I—their long lost "sister" and outside child—showed up that they would give me a loving response. It is true I can't say it would never happen, but I feel it would be highly unlikely. What would be the point anyway? Yes, I may learn some information about health issues, behavior patterns, or that I look like him, but that's not important to me right now. Maybe someone can convince me there's a good reason to look him up.

I can't say that it's impossible he still might be alive and want to share his memories of the conversation he had with Shirley when she learned she was pregnant—if that conversation really happened. I'm also willing to admit that it could be possible that the conversation did not happen because Shirley didn't have any ideas that she and this man could have a future together or keep their baby. She told me her family would never have accepted a Black man into their family and would put her out if they knew about him, which is what Agnes' father had done with her. Therefore, why would she tell him she was pregnant? I never thought to ask Shirley that question. I wish I could now.

I think it is possible that he didn't know about me (the embryo). But if he had known, what evidence is there that he would have wanted to have the baby or that he would now be thrilled to meet and claim me as his "daughter?" If I traveled along that line of thinking, I would be entering a fantasyland for no reasonable purpose. Maybe if I had grown up in an orphanage, barely educated, suffering from poverty, or feeling rejected by never being adopted, meeting a man who might say he would've reversed that experience had he known would be a good reason to seek him out. But my life was very enchanted despite the traumatic experience I had for six weeks when I was five years old. I haven't grown up wishing I were born into a united, wonderful family of love and acceptance because I did! I believe I was delivered to that family, only by another source.

My mother and I used to talk about the possibility that if she hadn't miscarried ten months into her marriage to my father, the pregnancy could've delivered me to them. But she couldn't carry me, so God sent me to them via Shirley. She believed that was possible and so do I.

Nevertheless, I may do some investigating about my biological father as encouraged by my daughter and my dear friend, Nadine, to see what information I can find. I would not be seeking a new or different "daddy," but he might turn out to be an interesting individual.

My beloved father Andrew lived to be nearly 89 years of age. He was a fabulous father. He guided me to love people, treat everyone equally, and to never see myself as better than or less than anyone. He made me feel secure and safe as a child, and he listened to me endlessly. He taught me to feel free, how to dance, understand harmony in music and in life, and he encouraged me to follow my dreams. I disappointed him by dropping out of college, but he understood that I had the ability to acquire additional education when the time was right for me. He was my biggest champion when I returned to college, and made sure I had the support that I needed. He loved his grandchildren and eagerly agreed to provide care for them every summer of their childhood. He and my mother took them to camp, swimming, on trips around New England, and made sure they were happy and safe.

My father developed Alzheimer. When he realized his mind was slipping away, he made sure that he told me how much he loved me, how proud he was of me as a person and as a mother, and that he wanted me to always remember that—and I do.

My father made his transition on December 6, 1991. He lived on earth long enough to know that I had completed my Doctorate at the University of California – Berkeley in May of 1991. He attended Cole and Robin's college graduations, and he knew that she had completed Law School which also occurred in May of 1991. So when people ask me about my real father, this is what I tell them.

Andrew on his way to church where he sang in the choir, 1985

CHAPTER TWELVE
Agnes and Shirley

I have shared that Shirley and Agnes had planned to remain friends, and they had thought they could arrange for me to grow up knowing Shirley. Well, that didn't happen. Once I connected with Shirley, I learned that these two women did speak to each other at least once per week on the telephone for 50 years until Agnes couldn't speak anymore. I also began to understand why my mother was so worried about me meeting Shirley. Agnes was a very dynamic and aggressive person. She was a loving parent, but she wasn't affectionate or soft. She was more direct, somewhat demanding, often intimidating, and very volatile. She would say, "Hey! I'm Italian…we shout!" I never doubted she loved me more than anything and anyone else in the world, but she wasn't the type of person to come up and hug you, which is something I needed and she knew that.

Agnes knew I had a quiet nature and was affectionate. I also loved harmonious interactions, which was always difficult for her. She also knew that Shirley was affectionate, sensitive, and easy going. She never raised her voice or seemed angry about anything. I believe Agnes worried that Shirley's kind and soft demeanor would appeal to me.

Agnes underestimated how much I loved her, and that I felt that she and no one else was my mother—the mother I was supposed to have. No matter how affectionate Shirley may have been, Agnes was the one who made sure I was legally adopted and protected from the busybodies. She made sure I was well educated and informed about my heritage and history. She taught me to stand up for what I believed in, to have the courage of my convictions, and to hold my head up proudly. She never had a thing to worry about because I wasn't going anywhere with Shirley or anyone else.

My mother lived to be 78, and made her transition April 4, 1996. She knew that my daughter had married a nice man in 1994 and was pregnant with a baby that was due on Christmas Day, 1996—the day he was born. I know if my mother still had the power of speech, she would have proudly said, "My grandson-in-law is a doctor! And my great-grandson is a Christmas baby!"

She knew when Cole was going to complete college, and she made sure to be at both of her grandchildren's college graduations. She knew they would accomplish the goals they set for themselves, which they have done. Cole graduated from Boston University School of Social Work with a Master degree and is a very successful Social Worker specializing in Gerontology and is very loved and appreciated by all of the senior citizens he helps. Robin is an extraordinarily excellent Labor Attorney. The employees who report to her admire and respect her, praising her for all that she teaches them. Cathy, the one and only one who I call my sister, lives in Connecticut and owns her business as a landscaper/photographer. She is a very gifted multi-media artist. The main thing I regret is that my parents made their transition before my fabulous grandson Christopher came into this world. But who knows, maybe they sent him to us. Christopher is a loving, caring, warm and thoughtful young man. He is extremely smart like his mother and father and ambitious in his career as a Marketing Representative in the entertainment field. He graduated from the University of Southern California—with a job! He makes everyone in our joint family extremely proud, and keeps us laughing with his terrific sense of humor. My parents would absolutely love him.

– # –

Shirley had been the chief caregiver for her aged parents and older siblings. She spent hours providing care for her family members, and she expected the same type of care when she got older. However, as she aged she felt her grandson, Danny, no longer wanted to spend time with her though she understood this was normal for a teenager. She also expressed to me that she felt her two surviving sons didn't spend enough time with her. Shirley became depressed during the last five years of her life. It is very sad, but it seemed to me that she mostly willed herself away.

Shirley O'Mara Cushen made her transition January 17, 2010. She was a Capricorn, like my grandson, Christopher, and she had just had her 88th birthday that December. Unfortunately, her son Michael died almost exactly one year after she died. I hope her twin sons are with her in the hereafter.

There is no question that my divine Guardian Angels protected me and made sure that while I may have come into this life via another woman's body, my life began with the most perfect parents and the blessings bestowed upon me throughout my life are nothing less than glorious. Twice, as a result of head injuries, I was pronounced dead on arrival at major hospitals in Boston. However, the medical staff was mistaken because here I am still living my life. During those experiences I saw the "white light" one hears about and believe I got to those pearly gates, but the Angels sent me back both times. There must be something important in this life that they wanted me to do. Hopefully, this book is one of those things.

June saying goodbye to the Oakland/San Francisco Bay on her PhD graduation day, Oakland, CA, 1991

CHAPTER 13
"In closing..."

Well, this is the story of my adoption. Of course, there are many more details —too many to include. But overall, what you've read is basically what happened.

Many people have asked me, "What was it like to be adopted?" Overtime, I've learned that they expect to hear a sad story. I realized this because even though I tell them it's been wonderful, they still ask me questions like, "How long were you in an orphanage?" and "Did you ever want to find your birthparents?" or "Did you feel your parents favored your sister because she wasn't adopted?"

I understand that they have heard about adoption stories that include many negative experiences. I can only remind them that my adoption was a private one between my birthmother and my parents, which means that I never lived in an orphanage but went home with my parents straight from the hospital when I was five days old. I also didn't need to "find" my birthmother because she was in my hometown in constant contact with my parents although I do not know my birthfather or where he might be. However, that hasn't been an issue for me. And there was never a day in my life that I felt less loved or cherished by my parents than my sister or any other living soul.

Of course, if I hadn't left my home on a journey to Alabama but had stayed with my parents during the rest of Agnes' pregnancy and if they had managed to weave into my understanding not only that I would no longer be an only child but I was about to be the "best big sister" and that I was also "chosen" by them, it may have been a better solution to how I learned I was adopted. But I will never know. Once I did learn and then accepted the fact that I was adopted, I was also aware of the wonderful life I was living. I had two doting parents who always made me feel like I was the center of their world.

My response to the question, "What has it been like to be adopted?" surprises many people, but it is and has been nothing less than "wonderful." I am very aware of the extraordinary number of blessings that I have received throughout my life beginning with the very careful plans for my adoption and then how those plans were so meticulously carried out during my birthmother's pregnancy.

It has also occurred to me that it may have been the best thing that she didn't tell her husband about who my birthfather was or that he was Black or the plans she had made with Andrew and Agnes Murray to adopt me while she was pregnant. Her husband was very religious, and if he had more time to think about the situation he might have decided that the "right" thing to do was to keep me even if it caused him emotional and political difficulty based on the racism his family and Shirley's family exhibited. I shudder to think of what my life would have been like had that happened! So her difficulty in telling him and her fear of being harshly treated by him meant she didn't tell him until the day I was born. As she had feared, his reaction was anger. Fortunately, without a lot of time to think about what to do, he agreed to the adoption. Plus, I'm sure Agnes' power of persuasion and assertiveness created a situation for which he was totally unprepared. So, things worked out perfectly for me, which was another major blessing—maybe the second time out of millions of times throughout my life that "things" worked out perfectly for me.

It is true that how I learned I was an adopted child could have been handled differently. The efforts my parents were making about teaching me of my adoption beginning from my birth until I was four years old were moving along fine—until Agnes became pregnant. The advice she and my father received to stop telling me I was adopted and start preparing me for a sibling may have been based on good intentions. But before my sibling was born, I went on a traumatic journey. As traumatic as it was, I never thought I was sent away because I was adopted because I didn't know I was adopted when that journey occurred. It was traumatic because I was away from my parents and my home. I was also neglected, frightened, lonely, underfed, eaten by ticks, and made to feel unwelcome. But I never thought I was experiencing these things because I was an adopted child.

Once I recovered from that trauma, my life moved forward beautifully. The challenges I had in my life had nothing to do with me being adopted. The funny thing is that sometimes months or years would go by without me even thinking or remembering that I was adopted. I've had the experience of meeting people who have told me they were adopted and it would suddenly pop into my mind that *oh yeah, I was too*. And some people who may have been my friends for years have said, "June, you never told me you were adopted!" to which I would reply, "Yeah well, I guess it never came up…" Those friends will then tell me I don't seem to be an adopted person—again expecting the sad story filled with upsetting experiences, but that just hasn't been my life. I think the only thing that may fit in with their expectations versus my experiences is those years I lied to myself about wanting to meet my birthmother. I remember one friend, Henry LaFargue, who told me, "One day you will realize that you DO want to meet her and I hope it won't be too late." Well Henry, you were right and thank goodness it wasn't too late.

There is one psychological aspect that often shows up with adopted people and I've learned from being in psychotherapy a few times throughout my adulthood that I have some trouble with it. The issue is feeling as though I might not have enough. I was informed that this minor feeling of insecurity often comes with the self-knowledge of being adopted. It seems to be associated with a sense of loss or losing, possibly associated with the idea that one was given away. For example, I used to think that my habit of stock piling groceries was as a result of being the child of a depression-era mother. My mom had it hard during her childhood and her family was quite poor. Once she married my father, she never had to worry about having enough food. Still, she would shop for groceries as though the world might come to an end any day. I thought I had inherited that habit from her, but I have learned my tendency to hold onto things and to over-shop for groceries, clothing, or just about anything isn't hoarding—it's my sense of not having enough. One might ask *enough of what*? It seems the answer is not enough love. So I comfort myself with things. Knowledge of oneself is supposed to bring change. Well, I try to remind myself I have plenty of love and I don't need five jars of peanut butter, or six bottles of hand sanitizer, or ten boxes of tissues at any one time. It may be a primal need that I'm feeding, but I'm not sure. I do know that the psychotherapists that I've seen have shared with me that this is a very common tendency for adopted people. It may be a deeply buried fear or concern in my subconscious that conflicts with what I understand intellectually, but there's often a gap between what we understand intellectually and how we feel emotionally. So, I forgive myself and try to re-channel my shopping over-drive. I share my peanut butter.

Another aspect of my adoption seems to have influenced my life's philosophy and vocation. Many people have asked me why so much of my professional work has such a strong multicultural/multiethnic emphasis. I think the answer stems from the folks who have peopled my formative life as well as those in the village who nurtured me. I have already shared that Agnes was Italian American, formerly Catholic and Episcopalian by marriage. And I've pointed out that Andrew Murray was African American and Episcopalian, and his paternal grandmother was a Native American originally from Oklahoma. Shirley was Irish American and Catholic, and her husband Sidney was of Russian immigrant parents of the Jewish faith. My birthfather was African American but there was some indication that he may also have been of West Indian/Caribbean heritage. Even the name of the OB/GYN who delivered me contributed to this multiethnic/multicultural extraordinary story because his name was Louis Gentile.

What other choice for a field of study or career would I make? Of course, I would choose to raise my children in a multicultural/multiethnic city. And of course when I returned to college, I earned a double major studying American Studies (which included African American Studies and Women's Studies) then Psychology. For my MSW in Social Work, I chose to practice Family Therapy and did my Internship in a multiethnic/multicultural residential substance abuse treatment center. Finally, my PhD was earned in a multi-disciplinarian department—the Ethnic Studies Graduate program at U.C. Berkeley. All of the college courses I've taught have a multicultural/multiethnic focus. There's really no secret why these facts exist—my life's studies and work reflect my life's origin.

When reflecting on my life as an adopted child while writing this book, it became clear that what had far more influence on who I am today was the bias and racism I experienced beginning with my parents' family of origin, including Shirley and Sidney's parents, the bias I experienced as an adolescent from girls who resented my appearance, the discrimination I experienced as a child in elementary and high school from some classmates and their parents, and certainly by my teachers and career counselors, and then the experiences

I had as a college student in Boston in 1961 with my White dorm mates who asked me questions such as "do colored people still have tails?", and the forces of discrimination in the city. I remember my two Black dorm mates and I walking along Commonwealth Avenue one day when we saw an older White woman who was sweeping her doorway. She looked at us and stopped sweeping until we were right at the bottom of her stairs. Then with her full force, she swept the dust onto us then raised her fist at us. Although she didn't say anything, her behavior and body language characterize my experiences with racism in Boston.

While reflecting on my life as an adopted person, I came to the conclusion that racism has had the most impact on my life and on who I am today—not being adopted.

In 1943, my mommy and daddy adopted me. That multicultural/multiethnic couple established my destiny. I am eternally grateful to them, Shirley and Sidney, and the whole family village who loved me and set me on a very successful life course. Also, I can't close this book without thanking my Guardian Angels for protecting my body and soul throughout my life. I know it was them who guided me to Shirley and Agnes and Andrew.

THE END

Murray family re-union at the home of Uncle Charlie and Aunt Corinne Murray in New Bedford, MA, 1950

June and Cathy with Macy's Santa Claus, New York City, NY, 1949

June's sister Cathy, Santa Cruz, CA, 1982

June's sister Cathy, with Uncle Doug, Atlanta, GA, Sept. 1994

June's grandson Christopher Patton, modeling an outfit from Ghana, 1999

June's grandson and his parents, Robin and Frank, when Christopher became an Eagle Scout, Atlanta, GA, 2014

June with Christopher at "Grandparent's Day", Atlanta, GA, 2011

June with Christopher on his high school graduation day, Atlanta, GA, 2015

Christopher and his parents during his senior year at the University of Southern California, Los Angeles, CA, 2018

Cole and Robin on Easter Sunday,
Milford, CT, 1966

June's children Cole and Robin,
ages 3 & 4, Boston, MA, 1967

Cole and Robin, age 4 & 5 in New
York City, NY, 1968

Cole and Robin, New York City, NY, 1972

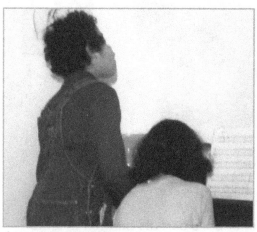

Cole and Robin playing the piano and
singing a duet, New York City, NY, 1973

Cole's high school graduation day
with Robin, Rochester, NY, 1981

Robin at 4 months, Boston, MA, 1964

Robin at 3 months during Christmas, 1964, Boston, MA

Robin on Easter Sunday, Milford, CT, 1967

Robin with her grandfather Andrew, Thanksgiving day, Milford, CT, 1967

Robin after graduation from Mills College, Oakland, CA, 1986

Robin on the day she was sworn in as a new attorney by Federal District Judge Erwin, Winston Salem, NC, 1991

June with Robin on her wedding day, Atlanta, GA, Sept. 1994

Robin in the Atlanta, GA K-9 race, 1998

Robin with son F. Christopher Patton, Atlanta, GA, 1998

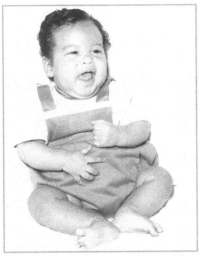

June's son Cole at 3 months, Boston, MA, 1963

Cole at 10 months, Boston, MA, 1984

Cole, age 7, at grandparents Murray's home, Milford, CT, 1970

Cole on his high school graduation day with his Murray grandparents, Rochester, NY, 1981

Cole as an undergraduate student at San Jose State University, San Jose, CA, 1985

Cole on his college graduation day, Oakland, CA, 1987

Robin congratulating brother Cole on his college graduation day, San Jose, CA, 1987

Cole on tour as a "Drum Tech" with the Stone Temple Pilots, 1990

Cole and family on the day of his graduation from the MSW program at the School of Social Work – Boston University, 2004

Cole, Washington, D.C., 2007

June and Cole, Las Vegas, NV, 2010

June with Cole, Robin and Christopher, Atlanta, GA, 2013

ACKNOWLEDGEMENTS

This is a book that I have been working on for at least 40 years—sometimes on paper and a lot of time just thinking through what I knew about it. As I said in the early chapters, the story of my adoption unfolded over many years. I learned about it from my parents, very close friends of the family, then from Shirley and her nephew, and finally from my DNA test. As the years went by, I talked about it many times. When people in my life learned that I was adopted, they asked me what the story was and I would tell them and include as many details as I could. There are valuable friends coast to coast who have heard the story; there is also my niece Philipina Kwashi in Ghana, West Africa, who adopted me as her "Aunti," who heard the story and always encouraged me "to write it down."

When the story was initially on my mind there were my adolescent friends Paula Wilson and Judy Imrie who were two of the first to listen and provide me with a great deal of emotional support. I remember telling the story to Tommy and Ginger Johnson, my Boston college pals and housemates, and they were also supportive. Over many years, Julette Johnson has also listened very intently and made encouraging comments about her feelings that I should definitely write the story for others to learn from. I sincerely thank her for that encouragement. Friends in New York City like Henry and Marietta LaFargue listened and advised me to look into my birthparents. Other NYC friends include Mercedes Rosas and Fabienne Kirk who always wanted me to write this book. I thank you for the urgings. There were friends in California and Durham, NC, many students in the classes I taught, and clients in my mental health practice who listened to my adoption story as a means to help themselves cope with their own adoption story.

Of course, my colleague and my "almost other son" – Dr. T. Alexander Washington always encouraged me to write my story and praised my efforts. He like some of my other friends read the early version of my manuscript and made editorial suggestions especially on the topic of the big mystery that occurred when I was five years old. I am especially grateful to my mentor Ann Laury who was especially supportive and encouraging about my interest in writing this book. She read an early version of the manuscript and offered insightful suggestions. Another special friend who took the time to read an early version of the manuscript is Michael Duarte and his comments were also very helpful.

All along the way my children Cole and Robin have listened to my story, made suggestions about writing the story, and offered their advice about the mystery. My friends in Charleston—Angela and Tony Burke, Amanda Bines, Alada Shinault-Small, and Deborah Agbor-Tabi—have been very patient as they listened to the story several times. I appreciate their support to keep focused on writing it all down. A special thank you to photographer John Singletary of Charleston who made it possible to include my grandfather George T. Murray's 1896 engagement photo.

Of course, this book would have never been completed if it weren't for the diligent attention, patience, support, and encouragement of my editor/publisher and great friend Nadine Johnson to whom I will always be grateful. There are many others who have always encouraged me to write my story, telling me that it was fascinating and so unusual. I agree...so now it has been written. Hopefully, my story will inspire others to write about their adoption to share with many others.

ABOUT THE AUTHOR

Dr. June P. Murray

Dr. Murray is a Clinical Social Worker, who earned a Master degree at Columbia University – School of Social Work in NYC. She went on to earn another Master degree at the University of California – Santa Cruz in Psychology, then a Master Degree and PhD at the University of California – Berkeley in Psychology and Ethnic Studies.

Dr. Murray has taught in the Social Work, Psychology, and Gerontology Departments in many universities across the country including U. C. Santa Cruz, U. C. Berkeley, and the State University of North Carolina – Raleigh. She served as the Chair of the Social Work Program at NC A&T State University and Chair of the Gerontology Program at the University of Maryland – Morgan Campus. She is a Mental Health Professional, and has provided psychotherapy for numerous agencies via her private practice. Dr. Murray is also a Pro-Diversity Consultant, and has served on conference panels and has organized focus groups on diversity as well as suicide prevention.

Dr. Murray is the author of the book *Guess What? I Was Adopted*, which is designed for parents and their adopted child to read together. It tells the story of a little boy who learned he was adopted and how happy he was to share the news.

Dr. Murray is the mother of Cole M. Gill and Robin C. Patton, and the grandmother of F. Christopher Patton. She is also a proud member of Alpha Kappa Alpha Sorority, Inc.

CPSIA information can be obtained
at www.ICGtesting.com
Printed in the USA
BVHW011553250321
603355BV00004BA/58